Teaching Juniors

Ruth Beechick

ACCENT BOOKS

Denver, Colorado

ACCENT BOOKS
A division of Accent Publications, Inc.
12100 W. Sixth Avenue
P.O. Box 15337
Denver, Colorado 80215

Library of Congress Catalog Card Number: 80-68886

ISBN 0-89636-062-8

Contents

1 Sketch of the Junior Child

● *In this first chapter you will find important characteristics of juniors, with special emphasis on those that interest you as their teacher. A few teaching hints are sprinkled in too, because juniors and their learning cannot be separated.*

In the "red room," which really had only a red door, juniors were noisily engaged in several activities. Troy took his family's auto blanket from the cupboard where he had stashed it the week before. "Here," he said to Holly, draping the blanket around her, "you have to be Mary. Everybody else is ready. We could give our play today if you'll just be Mary." Chad was at the chalkboard drawing a series of pictures, stopping occasionally to read intently from his Bible on the table nearby. Three children were at the bulletin board arguing about a list of duties. "You made a new list. It's supposed to be my turn today." "We had to. The old list got lost, and you just got the juice last week. It's not fair to have your name on almost every week." Julie was sorting attendance cards, pulling one out of the absent pocket and moving it to the present pocket each time someone came in.

Mrs. Holmes, who had been there earlier, but who often seemed as busy around the church as her children were, returned and began quietly to bring the class to order. "Thank you, Julie, for doing the attendance. How about holding the cards for a few more minutes until we're sure everyone's here?" "Are you almost ready, Chad? You can take a couple more minutes to finish. We'll have you first and then the play." "Is your play today?" she asked Troy.

"Yes, if Holly will be Mary. She says she doesn't know what to do."

"Oh, she'll be Mary. You know that story, Holly, and they'll help you if you need it. Why don't you all sit down now? We'll watch your play right after we listen to Chad's story."

Meanwhile, over in the orange room a class of juniors sat primly in a circle of chairs waiting for their teacher. This teacher was out for a moment, too, directing visitors. One empty chair waited for her, and the attendance materials were on it. The secretary stuck her head in the door, surveyed the scene, and said, "Why doesn't one of you do the attendance while you're waiting?"

"Oh, she wouldn't want us to do that," answered three or four children all at once.

Mrs. Reynolds returned, picked up the attendance cards, and sat down.

"Libby," she read.

"Present."

"Becky."

"Present." . . .

Classes develop their own distinctive personalities, just as individuals do. Part of the personality difference between the red and orange classes above was due to the difference in teachers, but not all. Mrs. Holmes may try to get her next year's class interested in plays, but it may not work at all. They may only seem interested in books. Mrs. Reynolds may try to get next year's class to be as docile and take all direction from her, but she may have someone like Chad, who was originally active and noisy in class and couldn't take much direction from anybody, but his outstanding art talent came to the rescue. It was his own idea one Sunday to draw a series of pictures illustrating a story, and the teacher didn't tell him to erase the board and sit down. She and his classmates admired the pictures and listened to him tell about them. "I'm going to do a story every Sunday," he announced. And so it became a regular feature in the red room. If Chad had been in the orange room you can be sure the children would not all have been sitting so primly. His busy mind would have stirred up some kind of commotion for them.

Though children and classes are quite individualistic, there are certain generalizations which can be made about junior children in groups. A generalization may not be true for all children in your class, but it is likely to be true for several or most of them. In this chapter, we present some of the major generalizations, which provide a good sketch of the junior child.

The junior child from ages 9 to 12 is in a period of generally good health. He does not tire as easily and is not prone to as many diseases as the primary child. His growth is slower and he seems to be in a period of consolidating his gains. He will work long and diligently at perfecting physical skills. Toward the end of this period many girls show a spurt of growth, and for a time they are taller than boys.

The junior becomes competitive. If there is a way to time or measure not only his running and jumping but his hobby and academic pursuits as well, he can be highly motivated through this means. But this ability of seeing his progress and achievement can work in reverse, too. The junior also sees his deficiencies. Thus he comes into the age of the inferiority complex, and parents and teachers have the important job of building his self-confidence.

In mental development, most juniors can reason about concrete matters. This is called today the "concrete operational stage" of thinking. Older juniors begin to reason about some abstract matters, but they are not yet moved into the stage of abstract thinking. These stages of thinking—concrete and abstract—are described more fully in Chapters 4 and 5.

Most children have mastered reading and writing so that these are now tools to use for social and recreational life and for learning. A child who cannot read by his early junior years is at a great disadvantage. The problem should be tackled with every means available. In our culture this is necessary for his self-confidence. He must be shown that he can learn, and to do this he must be making progress in learning. The few children who cannot learn to read by this time need much special help to face their limitations and to see their worth as individuals. It takes sensitive teachers to save these children from psychological damage.

For most children reading and writing are left behind, and arithmetic learning moves to center stage. When children tell their favorite subject or the subject they learn most in, they often mention math or science. Some, of course, mention gym or art. A few mention spelling. They like spelling if they do well, and they can easily measure week by week if they are doing well. Hardly anyone mentions reading or writing as a favorite subject or as one where he learns most. This shows the status of these subjects now as tools rather than as new skills exciting in themselves, as was the case in the primary years.

But though the children may not realize it, their teachers realize that there is still a long way to go in reading achievement. From this time on every teacher should be a reading teacher. Reading cannot be relegated to school reading periods but must be taught in all subject areas. In the subject of Bible, too. Juniors can make great strides in learning the specialized vocabulary for reading, writing and talking about the Bible. But this doesn't happen if the Bible teacher waits for the school reading teacher to teach words like sacrifice, prophet, or Nicodemus.

Juniors read voraciously, probably more than at any other period of life. Boys read boys' books and girls read both boys' and girls' books. The research on that has remained constant for many decades. Modern anti-sexist pressures on publishers and schools have done nothing to change reading tastes of the children themselves. Children love adventure, mystery, biography. Biographies of heroes in sports, history, and missionary work can have significant influence on the lives of juniors. Through heroes these children learn the qualities of greatness. They can identify with heroes who have overcome handicaps and who have achieved and have shown courage. With help, the children can see more of what makes for greatness. They can see that they have these qualities themselves and should work on developing them. It makes little difference whether the books are colorful. When there is art, children prefer it to be realistic. Highly stylized art may be chosen by those who work with children, but not by the children themselves.

Though the majority of junior children read many things, they tend to read what is easily available. Most do not go out of their way hunting up good reading. For churches, this says to bring the children's library right into the junior department. Allow book checkout time in the schedule and make it as routine as attendance taking. Special summer reading programs and other promotions can encourage more reading and keep children so busy with wholesome books that they have little time for other kinds.

Girls write somewhat better than boys. Few juniors do well in overall organization of essays. With good teaching, they can write adequate sentences and work on organizing one paragraph well.

If a child is endowed with exceptional amounts of any aptitude this often is evident in early junior years.

TEACHING JUNIORS

By later junior years the special aptitudes are more generally apparent. The innate basic elements of musical aptitude are as good as they probably ever will be. Many children begin music lessons during junior years, and this seems timed about right. Children with exceptional musical aptitude could begin earlier.

By the end of the junior years, children have as clear a grasp as most adults do of many musical concepts, and that is not a very high level. Terms like *steps, skips, phrase, melody,* and *harmony* are not used correctly by most people, according to the National Assessment of Educational Progress. Knowledge of musical notation is also rather limited. Although many can identify clef signs, note names, sharps and flats, few know that two eighth notes are equivalent to a quarter note. Few can detect differences between what they hear and what they see on a score. In other words, people have obtained some "naming" learning, or information learning, on these matters but there is not good understanding or good ability to use this information.

Junior music teachers may interpret all this to mean that they do their job quite well at junior level, but nothing much is done beyond that age to carry the learning further. Or they may see it as a challenge to do even more, since for many people musical education ends about this time, as music courses beyond this age are usually elective. In our graded choirs we should consider how much emphasis to give to performance and how much to give to raising the level of children's basic musical understandings. Also we should consider the value of using songbooks in settings like the Sunday school. With books, occasional music reading instruction could be given along with spiritual instruction about the meaning of the words. This opportunity is missed when we always use only memory or use song charts or song sheets with only the words. The song sheet practice also often violates copyright laws, and we need to set a good example for our children in this ethical matter.

Junior children, especially boys, will sing too loudly if the song leader encourages this, but it is not good for their developing voices. One leader said, "I like your voices, boys, but that's too loud." After that the singing had a better musical sound and the boys did not harm their voices.

Art aptitude of juniors develops rapidly. If skill doesn't keep pace children become so critical of their own efforts that they lose interest in trying. When art instruction is provided, great progress is made during the ages from 9 to 13. Children who do artwork outside of school show greater increase in skill than those who do not. Classes and club activities of the church could provide some of this extra experience for children who show interest in art.

Mechanical aptitude and others also appear during these years. Children will try almost anything, but they need a free atmosphere for exploration. If their first efforts are to be tested, graded, or otherwise held up for public display they lack confidence. The time for competition in any activity is later, after the children know they can do it.

Juniors can work purposefully and with good attention for long periods. But on many projects they need guidance to produce something they will be proud of. It is a sensitive area to know when to give help and how to give it, because children can feel threatened, as though they are not considered capable. Juniors very much need teaching in practically all areas of their lives, but they need to feel this teaching is bringing out their abilities rather than pointing up their deficiencies.

Memory abilities of juniors are good. Teachers are right to take advantage of this, but they should guard against overdoing it to the neglect of other kinds of learning.

Juniors move forward in social skills. They are able to

see others' viewpoints and feelings so they are capable of true sympathy. Their insecurities and clumsy social skills, however, often make them appear thoughtless. The teaching approach here is highly effective. Instead of constantly meting out punishments for children's verbal quarrels, bullying tactics, and so forth, teachers accomplish more by showing good ways to act. The teacher must model proper behavior. If one child is the object of teasing or aversion, the teacher can work wonders by genuinely appreciating that child's unique contribution to the group. If he appreciates good things in the teasers, too, and in everyone else in the class, the children catch this from the teacher. They learn to appreciate each other and they learn the skill of expressing it.

So it is with all social skills; children learn from the teacher's modeling. They also learn from direct teaching. If there is to be a wedding the teacher can explain to the children how to go through the reception line and what to say. They might practice this. If there is a cookie social, the class can practice again, and talk about how people wait in line, take only a couple of cookies, walk about carefully because people are holding cups of punch, and so forth. Cookie monsters may not become cookie angels overnight, but progress can be made through the junior years. The children do need someone to explain to them how to act in various situations.

The child who is not developing socially, as the typical junior, can become a big problem. He may be aggressive and quite disturbing to his teachers and classmates. Often the first approach should be for the teacher to try to channel such a child's energy into useful activities. Repressing his energy seldom works. If the problem persists and grows, more adults should be enlisted to help solve it. It is urgent to help troubled juniors because it is so much easier than helping the troubled adolescents that they will become.

The frightened, withdrawn child also needs loving

help. But we must be careful not to classify too many children as either too boisterous or too quiet. There is a wide range of normalcy. It is not a sin to be a quiet "loner." God uses all kinds of personalities.

Gangs and clubs are the trademark of junior ages, and these provide lots of practice in getting along with others. Churches capitalize on this characteristic by offering boys' and girls' clubs during these years. Sunday school classes take on club-like features, too, by having projects, contests, and social times. Churches which make good use of clubs can easily hold children through the junior years.

Same-sex clubs are the rule. When children form their own clubs they are of one sex only. Gangs are formed spontaneously. Leadership changes according to the immediate purpose. Whoever has an idea and knows how to carry it out is leader for the time being. Classes need not be segregated by sex, though. Junior children are used to mixed classes at school. These work well in church also.

Pets become important, and "best friends," too. Children develop their natural sympathy and affection through these. They need more help in transferring this feeling to brothers and sisters at home. They are capable of planning ways to make their homes happier and can carry out some projects of this type.

Juniors show strong concern about fairness, and insist on rigid adherence to rules. These characteristics have been described as Stage 2 in a scale of moral reasoning. (See Chapter 3.) In their better moments juniors are capable of understanding reasons for things that at first look unfair. They can appreciate, for instance, that a child who has a hard time learning should not be held to such high standards as a child who learns easily. They can understand the higher principle that God wants each person to do his best with what he has.

Other higher principles are also within reach of

juniors. They can recognize that God runs His universe on laws of righteousness. They can see advantages in living according to God's will.

On the stages of faith developed by James Fowler, most junior children are Stage 2, called the "mythic-literal" stage. This is when the person begins to take on for himself the stories, beliefs and observances of his own community. This would be the church community if he and his family are sufficiently immersed in it. The junior child adopts the rules and attitudes of this community. He takes on its beliefs—with literal interpretations. Parental authority and example are important, still counting more than pressure from peers.

Juniors like teachers who make them work, who expect and get good behavior from the class members, and who are businesslike in their classroom and teaching manner. Those qualities are mentioned most often in surveys. Also mentioned are qualities of kindness, patience, fairness, helpfulness, friendliness, openminded-ness. Children like teachers who know their subject, who are interested in the pupils, and who have a sense of humor. And they like their teachers to not be sarcastic or nagging.

When teachers are surveyed about children they tend to think that character traits are slipping from what they used to be. A good many teachers cite television as the main villain. They report that children are only half awake in school, their attention spans are shorter, and they lack persistence. If a job takes very long, children will not complete it. They want instant gratification. Children are not as self-directive as they used to be, say these teachers, and their imaginations are stunted. They simply wait to be told what to do.

Moreover, these TV children relate to others poorly. They settled disputes with martial arts when a popular program taught them this. They indulge in name-calling and put-downs, as several popular shows do. They have lost feeling for a child hurt on the playground, and one ill at home is quickly forgotten. They are lonely, and know TV as their most faithful companion who sends them to school, greets them upon their return and is a third parent to them.

Some schools have developed plans which encourage a restricted TV diet and find that children become more relaxed and more imaginative. They smile again and quarrel less. Play, conversation and companionship do more for these children than TV does.

Other surveys show that there is more use of tobacco, liquor and drugs than formerly. Environment of home and friends has a lot to do with who gets involved. Children from loving, disciplined homes with sure values may experiment with forbidden evils, but at junior ages they do not easily leave their home culture or lifestyle for another.

This has been a sketch of the junior child's physical, mental, and social growth. Physically, in his size and strength, he is growing slowly. But his physical skills are developing by leaps and bounds, as are also his mental skills. His social skills are coming along too—not quite leaping, but plodding.

Now, what about the spiritual growth of the child? In his Christian education this is more important than any other area. This aspect of the child is considered in the next chapter. Then the two following chapters describe in more detail the moral and mental development of the child, which were sketched briefly here.

READING CHECK

1. Juniors are in a period of rapid physical growth.

T F

2. Juniors can be motivated by competition.　T F
3. Juniors can be discouraged by competition.　T F
4. Most juniors have completed learning how to read.

T F

5. Juniors' musical aptitudes are about as good as they will ever be. T F

6. Children's art abilities develop naturally without special teaching. T F

7. Juniors have short attention spans. T F

8. Typical juniors like gangs and clubs. T F

9. Juniors often show strong concern for fairness. T F

10. Juniors like teachers who are ''easy'' and let them get by with most anything. T F

Answers: 1–F, 2–T, 3–T, 4–F, 5–T, 6–F, 7–F, 8–T, 9–T, 10–F

2 Spiritual Development

● *In this chapter you can try to understand the mystery of your spiritual self with the help of Franz Delitzsch, a theologian of the 1800s. You will read, too, what "reductionist" psychologies are. You don't want that kind. You want the spiritual kind. In the latter part of this chapter you will read about spiritual developmental tasks. You will become acquainted with a list of these and come to understand how the list works.*

A fifth grade Sunday school teacher starting out with her brand new class in the fall wanted a quicker than usual way to find out what her children understood about salvation. And she wanted to find out which children claimed to be saved. So she devised a brief questionnaire for the children to fill out in class. Fourteen children had answers similar to the first example below, and one child answered as in the second example.

What does it mean to be saved?

It means Jesus is in your heart

How does a person become saved?

He asks Jesus into his heart

Are you saved? *yes* Tell about it.

One day when I was seven years old, my mom told me if you except Jesus into your heart you will be saved. So I excepted him into my heart.

What happens when someone dies?

He goes to heaven if he is saved.

What does it mean to be saved?

Someone saves your life

How does a person become saved?

Are you saved?   Tell about it.

Your cought between a fire and someone helps you get out.

What happens when someone dies?

they tryed but didn't sucede or you didn't helps.

This assessment took only three or four minutes of class time, and the teacher then could see clearly what teaching was needed for one boy in her class. But not much was clear yet for the other fourteen, except that they badly needed some spelling instruction. In the following weeks through discussions and other interactions with the children she came to know each child better and to see what she might be able to teach them.

In the spiritual realm probably more than any other, we rely on our self-knowledge and our common sense. Often we feel we just know what the children need. And most of the time we probably are right. Certainly our common sense tells us more than science does about these matters. To sharpen thinking we will examine spiritual development in this chapter from two different viewpoints. First, we will consider some things the Bible has to say about spirit, and about man as a spiritual being. Secondly, we will look at a list of spiritual developmental tasks. This list shows what we can expect students to achieve at various ages during their growth.

Franz Delitzsch has given us a good, biblical picture of man, in *A System of Biblical Psychology* (first published in 1855, reprinted in English in 1977 by Baker, Grand Rapids). He explains that man has a unique position between the spiritual and the earthly. He is not purely spiritual, and he is the highest of the earthly (Psalm 8). He is the connecting link between the two. He is of the earth, yet God breathed from Himself the spirit of life into him (Psalm 10:18; Genesis 2:7).

When God breathed the spirit of life into Adam, he became a living soul, so the principle of life can be viewed on one side as spirit and on the other as soul. This breath of life from God is the original cause of both bodily life and spiritual life. Scripture sometimes speaks of body and spirit (James 2:26), sometimes of body and soul (Matthew 10:28), sometimes it differentiates between soul and spirit (Hebrews 4:12), and sometimes it uses all three terms together (I Thessalonians 5:23).

It is abundantly clear from Scripture that there is a spiritual aspect to man. This is where our Christian psychology differs from others. It gives a central place to all that is spiritual in man—the heart, conscience, soul, personality, mind, and any other aspects which are not material or physical. We look at man from above, so to speak, while other psychologies look at him from beneath. The psychologies that describe man from beneath are called "reductionist psychologies." Reductionists try to understand complicated concepts by lower level concepts. They try to explain man in terms of physiology. Then they explain physiology in terms of chemistry, then chemistry in terms of molecular behavior, and so forth. From man down to molecules. The lower levels are regarded as more fundamental, and thus able to actually explain the higher levels. Many psychologists, particularly behaviorists such as B. F. Skinner, believe that man will eventually "dissolve," as they come to understand from the material side just what he is made of. This is reductionist psychology. Reduce man to molecules and less.

Instead of a reductionist psychology, ours is a creationist psychology. We believe God created us in His image. We explain from above and not from below.

What does it mean to be created in the image of God? Delitzsch explains that God is light and love and spirit, so Adam must have been given all of these. And when he sinned, his spirit could not dissolve into elements, as the body does, because spirit is not composed of elements. Spirit was not annihilated, because we see that God did not do this in the case of evil spirits, whose sin is such that it is incapable of redemption. So what happened to the spirit in man at his fall? It became possessed by death. The spiritual life in God's image was dead. Where God's love had filled the spirit's will and thought and feeling, where God's image had been reflected in the soul, where

God's peace had reigned, now the spirit had fallen away from all this. The glory was gone. Soul came under the power of natural self instead of under the spirit. Confusion and shame and fear took hold of man.

Fear, even Satan and his angels have. But shame and guilt are our advantage over them. Without shame and guilt we could not come back to God. This conscience is the "remains" of spirit in us. This is the point of entrance for the Word which we lay hold of by the faith produced by that Word. When the Word enters, the conscience is purged (Hebrews 9:14; 10:22). We are thus reborn and God's work of grace begins in us to restore again the image of God which we had lost.

Spiritual growth, then, is a work of God's grace. Almost every letter of the New Testament closes with the writer saying to his fellow believers something like, "The grace of our Lord Jesus Christ be with you all." Growth in grace is seen to be of major importance. Peter admonished his readers to "grow in grace, and in the knowledge of our Lord and Savior Jesus Christ." He told them to desire the milk of the Word for their growth. Paul wanted his hearers to graduate from milk and get on to meat. Growth comes by the Word of God through the grace of God.

One who has suffered much for Christ under communism, and who has seen much suffering in others, has said that there are two ways to grow—by suffering and by the Word. Growth by suffering can be seen in Paul's writing (Philippians 3:8-11). But since we do not use that method in our teaching of children, we are left with the Word.

Everyone needs the Word. Those who are dead spiritually need the Word to give them faith. Those who have been reborn need the Word to enable them to grow. So our teaching job in the spiritual realm boils down to being the best teachers of the Word that we know how to be. In this chapter are some suggestions which hopefully are not too tainted by the reductionist psychologies of the day.

We must remember that our educational programs are not synonymous with spiritual development. That is, the development doesn't happen because we take children by the hand, or the hickory stick, and lead them through the proper steps. Their development is happening anyway by the grace of God, and we merely try to fit in.

Fitting in with the junior years means being a strengthening influence for fragile plants. Paul said that those who are tossed to and fro, carried about with every wind of doctirne, are like children (Ephesians 4:14). He admonished the Ephesians to be perfected and built up and grown up—not to be like children. The figure is apt because children are easily tossed about by teachings. Junior children quite readily pick up the strangest of ideas about the spirit world or about heaven and hell or what happens after death—or before birth (i.e., former lives)—if they are exposed to these ideas through friends, books, movies, or popular records.

Children need dependable adults close by to guide them through this time. They need all the doctrinal teaching we can manage through these years, and very little that's in the Bible should be considered inappropriate for learning in the junior years. Foundations for most major doctrines should already be laid. Juniors should already have a good biblical view of the doctrines of God, Jesus, the Holy Spirit, sin, salvation, heaven, hell, death, angels, Satan, demons, creation, future things, and the Bible. These all can be taught at a concrete level to primaries, as explained in the primary book of this series. Doctrines of the church are more difficult to teach at primary age, so juniors may have only seen the church in two or three Bible stories and learned the rest of what they know by seeing their own church and its missionary outreach in action. Junior children are not so tied to learning by stories as they were at primary ages, so they are now able to handle a good unit of study on biblical doctrines of the church and the important distinctives of their own church. The other doctrinal learnings should also be reinforced and built up throughout the junior years.

The curriculum need not be organized around doctrinal teachings if that kind of organization was used during primary years. But if it wasn't, juniors need good units of study built around important doctrines. An organization that uses historical and chronological "big ideas," as described in Chapter 8 could also be used. In this, doctrines will come up in different kinds of contexts, and juniors' understanding will continue to grow.

In considering a child's total spiritual development there is a wide range of matters to keep in mind. We can easily be led to an imbalance in one direction or another because so much of research and writing on education concerns mental development or psychological development, and as we give attention to these things that have been written about so much we may neglect other equally important, or even more important, areas. To help give a balance, we propose here a list of spiritual developmental tasks.

The idea of developmental tasks was made prominent by Robert Havighurst in the 1950s. Havighurst's tasks included biological, psychological and social development. In the years since the publication of his list, curriculum planners and teachers have made much use of it. But the list omits the spiritual aspect, as Havighurst himself noted.

This list of spiritual developmental tasks was derived in the Havighurst manner. The total list is given, as it is important to know what comes before junior age and what comes after it, as well as what is particularly timely during junior years. In other words, we need the horizontal look at what happens during one period of a child's life and we also need the vertical look at what happens across ages as he grows. This is explained in more detail following the list itself.

LIST OF
SPIRITUAL DEVELOPMENTAL TASKS

Spiritual Developmental Tasks of Preschool
1. Experiencing love, security, discipline, joy, worship.
2. Beginning to develop awareness and concepts of God, Jesus, and other basic Christian realities.
3. Developing attitudes toward God, Jesus, church, self, Bible.
4. Beginning to develop concepts of right and wrong.

Spiritual Developmental Tasks of Elementary School Years
1. Receiving and acknowledging Jesus Christ as Savior and Lord.
2. Growing awareness of Christian love and responsibility in relationships with others.
3. Continuing to build concepts of basic Christian realities.
4. Learning basic Bible teachings adequate for personal faith and everyday Christian living, including teachings in these areas:
   a. prayer in daily life.
   b. the Bible in daily life.
   c. Christian friendships.
   d. group worship.
   e. responsibility for serving God.
   f. basic knowledge of God, Jesus, Holy Spirit, creation, angelic beings, heaven, hell, sin, salvation, Bible history and literature.

5. Developing healthy attitudes toward self.

Spiritual Developmental Tasks of Adolescence
1. Learning to show Christian love in everyday life.
2. Continuing to develop healthy attitudes toward self.
3. Developing Bible knowledge and intellectual skills adequate for meeting intellectual assaults on faith.
4. Achieving strength of Christian character adequate for meeting anti-Christian social pressures.
5. Accepting responsibility for Christian service in accordance with growing abilities.
6. Learning to make life decisions on the basis of eternal Christian values.
7. Increasing self-discipline to "seek those things which are above."

Spiritual Developmental Tasks of Maturity
1. Accepting responsiblity for one's own continued growth and learning.
2. Accepting biblical responsibilities toward God and toward others.
3. Living a unified, purposeful life centered upon God.

An important characteristic of this kind of list is that tasks at any one age level are usually found to develop together in people. Thus, you will seldom find juniors who do well in one or two tasks and poorly in others. They will do well in all or poorly in all or somewhere in between. For instance, you are not likely to find a junior child who has not received Christ as his Savior (Task 1) doing well in the other junior tasks. Nor are you likely to find a child with poor attitudes toward himself (Task 5) developing well in any of the other areas.

This means we must give attention to all areas. Our teaching cannot be badly out of balance. One way a teacher could unbalance it is to emphasize too heavily some current, faddish, psychological approaches to building self-concept. If this is done to the neglect of other areas, the neglected ones will not grow and neither will the self-concept. The areas grow together. They need each other. In this case, growth in Bible knowledge and doctrine, growth in Christian friendships, and so forth are all aids to a healthy self-concept.

Another way a teacher could unbalance the teaching is to emphasize the behavior type tasks to the neglect of important Bible knowledge the child should be gaining, or the building of his inner self. This might happen when there is too much adherence to the behaviorist theory, which demands only outwardly observable and measurable goals.

A second important characteristic of the list is that the tasks develop in order through the ages. For instance, the preschool concepts of right and wrong are a necessary foundation for salvation. And experiencing love at preschool age (Task 1) is necessary for school-age growth in showing Christian love (Task 2). This works in reverse, too. Thus if you have a school-age child who did not begin experiencing love in preschool years he will not develop normally in Christian love in his school years. You might say he is retarded in love. As a remedial teacher, then, you would have to begin at the beginning. Love him, and help him receive and experience love. Only then can he go on to the next step in love.

As a junior teacher you will appreciate parents and teachers who have helped your children with foundation learning at preschool and early school years. You will also see that what you teach in junior years is extremely important for the teen years that follow. For example, you need to do a good job of teaching Bible and Christian doctrine at junior level in order for the children in teen years to succeed at their Task 3. This task is, "Developing Bible knowledge and intellectual skills adequate for meeting intellectual assaults on faith." When our Christian education fails in this area, we have incidents of our church young people going off to universities and "losing their faith," as we describe it. A teen is not another kind of person. He is the continuation of the child in your junior class.

We have seen that the tasks at any one age are best developed together and that the tasks at each age are a necessary foundation for those at the next age. Now, a third characteristic of the list is that it defines an "optimum age" for teaching things. We readily see the optimum age principle in physical matters. For instance, doting parents may work and work at teaching their baby to walk, but the effort is wasted if the baby is not yet physically ready to walk. Physical maturity is one factor in determining optimum age. Other more complex factors are mental and psychological maturity, motivation or heart-set, and social pressures. Churches exert social pressure. If everybody is being confirmed or making a public profession of faith at a certain age, the social pressure motivates children to get busy and qualify too. This presents the "teachable moment" that we teachers like so much.

When the teachable moment is here we should take advantage of it. In a broader sense, that is what the optimum age principle is. It is taking advantage of the best time for teaching various things. If we try to teach juniors the intellectual skills of teens we waste our time. They are not mentally prepared for it.

Preschool age, even babyhood, is the optimum time for beginning to love children. If this love is delayed in a child's life all other development is crippled. Elementary school age is the optimum time for teaching how to

27

be saved. A great many children respond at this age— a few are saved earlier and some later. But the optimum time for this teaching seems to be the elementary school years.

So this list of tasks shows us 1) development across the ages, 2) interrelated areas of growth within each age, and 3) the optimum time for the various teachings with those who are growing normally.

If this list is used, either as it is or modified to suit your church, you can base many curriculum decisions on it. You can study it to see if there are areas you need to add to your juniors' learning. Are there things you try to teach that might better be left for the teen years? You might have the list in mind when you are selecting published lesson materials for your church. You can use it to help develop your own set of goals for the junior years. This is a tool, closer to the heart of Christian education than some.

READING CHECK

1. Our Christian common sense can tell us more about children's spiritual development than scientific research can.   T F

2. An unsaved person of accountable age is spiritually dead.   T F

3. The Word of God brings spiritual life and growth to junior children.   T F

4. Humanist psychologies can tell us much about the heart and soul of humans.   T F

5. The best way to explain how a child grows and develops is to use reductionist psychologies.   T F

6. Developmental tasks describe normal development in people who have reasonably good home and church learning conditions.   T F

7. A list of developmental tasks helps us see the best time to stress certain teachings.   T F

8. Developmental tasks help explain that learners can be highly developed in one spiritual area, but way behind in another. T F

3 Moral Development

• *In this chapter the theologian Delitzsch will explain to you just what conscience is, and the psychiatrist Bettelheim will agree with him. Then you must take a look at Lawrence Kohlberg's scale of moral reasoning, partly because everybody's talking about it now. Also, it really will give you some help, if you don't carry it too far.*

What does it mean to be moral? It means to do right instead of wrong.

Who knows best what is right or wrong? Christians.

When it comes to moral education, Christians have been doing it best all along. Our goals are clear. Our standard, the Bible, is absolute. We should not be confused at all about our work in teaching morals. The world around us is terribly confused at the present time. They are trying this and trying that in education in desperate attempts to improve the morality situation but we are the ones with the answers.

Much of the world's confusion comes from an inadequate view of man. In our Christian view we include the spiritual aspect of man. We include heart. Good and evil come from the heart, as we see in numerous Scripture verses (for example, Jeremiah 16:12; Psalm 32:11; I Kings 8:61; Matthew 12:34, 35). Conscience is seated in the heart (Romans 2:15; Hebrews 10:22).

Heart is the center of moral life. Thus we who believe in heart have the superior moral education. In this chapter we will look first at what the Bible says about conscience, being guided by Delitzsch's study of this topic. And next, we will look at the mental aspect of moral development as studied by Lawrence Kohlberg.

Conscience was built into man from the very beginning. When the serpent tempted Eve she answered that God had said not to eat of the fruit of the tree in the middle of the garden. She knew she shouldn't eat it. This was conscience. It warned, but Eve, and Adam, disregarded the warning, suppressed conscience, and disobeyed God. Here we see that conscience works before sin by warning. It works after sin, too, by bringing guilt. Adam and Eve were struck with shame and fear by their consciences, and they hid from God. This is the condition people are in now apart from God's grace. Their consciences tell them that they are guilty before God.

This conscience is part of man's nature, not of God's. It is not God's "voice" speaking to us, if by that we mean that God steps into our lives either continually or now and then to remind us about the way we should go. No, God created man in the beginning with conscience, and that is the "voice" that speaks to us. We were created with self-knowledge, and part of that knowldge is our relation to God. We know, as Eve did, what we should do or should not do in relation to God. Conscience is the knowledge of God's law written in our hearts (Romans 2:15).

With the law written in our hearts, conscience pricks and accuses. We can ignore the warning and hide from God, or we can heed the warning and come to God for release from guilt. If we come to God, He renews our consciences by His grace. Conscience is purged by the blood of Christ (Hebrews 9:14). The Christian, then, can serve God with a "good" conscience that does not accuse and bring guilt (Acts 23:1; I Peter 3:16,21; I Timothy 1:5,19; and others).

Conscience, in the Bible, is never said to be hard, but it may be seared, or branded, with false doctrine (I Timothy 4:2). And it may be weak due to lack of right knowledge. "There is not in every man that knowledge . . . and their conscience being weak is defiled" (I Corinthians 8:7). Throughout this passage to the Corinthians we see that conscience may waver and be in error. Thus it is not an infallible guide, as God's Law is, yet man is supposed to live by his conscience according to his measure of faith, "for whatsoever is not of faith is sin" (Romans 14:23).

We find, then, that conscience is innate to the child; it is part of his nature inherited from the first created human. And if parents (and teachers) discipline and teach according to God's plan, the child's given conscience will not become seared by false teaching or become weak from lack of right knowledge. The education needed seems not to be learning rules about what to do or not do, such as whether a certain kind of entertainment or a certain kind of meat is all right. This kind of knowledge is said to make a person arrogant or puffed up. Those who think they know these things really know nothing. To love God is the important thing (I Corinthians 8:1-3).

In the Corinthian church some had weak consciences, and Paul did not admonish the church to educate the weak members about idols and meat offered to them. Instead, he appealed to those who had more knowledge—and, presumably, stronger consciences—to change their behavior. He advocated behavior change for the strong, not the weak, or, we might say, for the teacher, not the taught!

Why this behavior change for the ones with knowledge? Possibly because they were puffed up. What they needed was love of God. If they displayed this love, the weaker ones could learn love too, and love was what they needed. Conscience is a matter of heart, not head.

The psychiatrist Bettelheim gives a view which is very close to this biblical view of conscience. Bettleheim does not recognize that conscience is innate, as the Bible teaches. But apart from that he has found through his psychiatric work much truth about conscience. He calls it the superego, as psychiatrists do, and he says it is formed early in life on the basis of fear. This conscience (superego) tells the young child what he can and cannot do, on the basis of fear rather than on the basis of reasoning. Yes, fear. This is the word that Bettelheim uses. The child fears punishment from his father. He knows at first by parental discipline what is right or wrong for him to do. As he grows, his mind (ego) slowly matures, his own reasoning gradually takes over, and he comes to live by a mature morality ("Moral Education" in *Moral Education/Five Lectures,* ed. Nancy F. and Theodore R. Sizer. Cambridge: Harvard University Press, 1970).

So moral learning, according to Bettelheim, has its basis in conscience. It cannot develop without conscience. In this he differs from most others these days who are making morality a cognitive matter. Moral teaching in schools consists of knowledge about drugs, the how-to of sex, the various options or lifestyles available to choose from, and so forth. To all the knowledge, children are supposed to apply reason, decide what they value, and decide how they will live. On some moral issues society has not yet given up its collective belief. For instance, honesty. Schools still want to teach children honesty, and our police system still provides some fear to help in this.

In Bettelheim's theory, not only moral learning but all of learning depends on the conscience which is first developed by fear. He says that without fear there can be no conscience, and without conscience there can be no learning. This is a remarkable teaching which is largely ignored by the modern world of educational psychology. The behaviorists and the humanists who have developed today's popular learning theories say nothing about this, but Solomon long ago said that the fear of the Lord is the beginning of knowledge and wisdom.

Bettelheim says in the essay cited above, "The mistake is that today too many believe that what ripe maturity can contain is therefore the best fare for immaturity. The mistake is to hope that more and more citizens will have developed a mature morality, one they have critically tested against experience, without first having been subject as children to a stringent morality based on fear and trembling."

Our old way was to instill fear of God and parents in the young child. The child feared to do wrong because of punishment which would follow. There was also a future orientation. The glories of heaven and the terrors of hell were in the future, but they built strong consciences. This future aspect is part of the "reality principle" of learning. With the reality principle, children work hard for results which are postponed. Conscience provides the motivation for this learning.

The new way, in contrast, uses the "pleasure principle." This is where learning is motivated by the pleasure it can give at the moment. This is not to say that reality learning is not often pleasurable. It is. But here we are contrasting two basic motivational forces. If the pleasure principle is the motivating force, then learning can happen only as long as it is pleasurable. But if the reality principle is the motivating force, then learning can happen even with long-postponed rewards. For Christians, with heaven in view, postponement of rewards is in the very nature of things. Christian learners are more solidly motivated.

Bettelheim advocates going back to the old ways of basing learning on fear. But he rejects fear of hell and of God, as being "crippling." He would substitute fear of losing parents' (or teachers') love at first, and later, the fear of losing self-respect. Some Christians will partially agree with this, feeling that the way we went about using fear in the past may have been crippling. But our answer to that charge should not be to throw out fears which worked so well in the past, and which are based on our firmly held truths anyway, but we should look into why and how they may become crippling. Perhaps fear only needs to be balanced with plenty of love. Many Christian parents, both in the old and the new days, have used fear and love in a successful combination. Their children grow up with good consciences, high motivation to learn, and well developed morality. As we said at the beginning of this chapter, Christians have done it best all along.

So for the answer to morality teaching the secular world should be looking to Christians instead of the other way around. Nevertheless, Christian educators have been watching what is happening in the fields of values education and moral education. The research of Lawrence Kohlberg, particularly, has caught the fancy of many in recent years. Kohlberg's idea was to free moral education from religion. He felt that if he could demonstrate a moral development that was separate from religious development he would have a basis for putting moral education back into the schools. His is a theory of moral *reasoning*.

In looking at Kohlberg's theory we need to keep that in mind. Heart is not in this theory, nor conscience, nor an absolute Bible standard of right and wrong, nor the high Bible standard of love. Standards come, instead, from what is found in the population studied. The highest standards that emerge are people's right to life and their right to just treatment in this life.

A brief look at this theory of moral reasoning is provided in the chart (Figure 1). To develop this description of stages and how people think at each stage, Kohlberg interviewed people about moral dilemmas. These are problems in which there is a choice between one value and another. One problem is the now well-known story of Heinz whose wife will die unless he steals the drug that can save her life. Here the values concerning theft and the druggist's right to his property are on one side. And the value of the woman's right to life is on the other. The actual choice the person makes is not scored, but his reasoning is scored at one of the stages given in the chart. If a person answers that Heinz should not steal because he will be put in jail for it, he is scored at Stage 1, as he is guided by the punishment consequences of the act. If he says that life should be saved even at the price of breaking the law because everyone has the right to life, he is scored at Stage 4, as he holds a high principle also held by society at large.

There seems to be no room for a Christian believer to answer along this line: "Heinz should pray and ask God what to do. God could provide the money for him to buy the drug. Or if He doesn't, it may be that the drug really will harm his wife in spite of what the doctors say. He should leave his problem in God's hands."

This "value" of Christian faith does not appear on the scale. Stage 6, the highest one, is individual conscience based on universal principles. But where do these principles come from? By the very nature of psychological research, these universal principles have to be derived from men and not from God.

The highest principle on Kohlberg's scale is "justice." In Socrates' conversation quoted from in Chapter 7, Socrates at one point says, "The last of those qualities which make a state virtuous must be justice, if we only knew what that was." He and Glaucon later arrive at a negative definition which sounds very much like the ten commandments. No one would steal or break agreements or commit adultery or dishonor father and mother. Socrates believed that this kind of living came from the inner life of a man at peace with himself—a man who is his own master and his own law. This sounds similar to what Kohlberg describes for his principled level.

PREMORAL LEVEL	STAGE 0. Does not understand or reason about moral issues. Has no conception of obligation to others or to authority. Good is what is pleasant, and bad is what is painful. Does what he can do or wants to do.
PRECONVENTIONAL LEVEL Responds to the way society labels good and bad or right and wrong, but only because of consequence to himself.	STAGE 1. Guided by punishment or reward consequences. Defers to authority or power not because of any respect for them but because avoiding punishment is a "good" in itself. STAGE 2. Guided by personal satisfaction and occasionally the satisfaction of others. Actions are a way to meet these needs. "You be good to me, and I'll be good to you." The fairness stage.

CONVENTIONAL LEVEL	STAGE 3. Guided by the expectations of others. Acts for the approval of others. The "good boy" stage.
Responds to society's expectations for reasons beyond himself—for loyalty.	STAGE 4. Understands something of the need for authority, rules, and social order. Respect for these is a "good." Duty is a good.
PRINCIPLED LEVEL	STAGE 5. Standards are social ones—those which have been evaluated and agreed upon by the whole society. But open to changing a law when it seems best to do so.
Tries to find values which have justification in their own right apart from any person or group which holds such a value.	STAGE 6. Standards are in the individual conscience rather than in laws or social agreements. Right principles are abstractions, such as justice, and are not concrete rules found in religions or philosophies or elsewhere.

Figure 1

(Adapted from "Moral Development and Moral Education in *Psychology and Educational Practice*, Ed. by G. Lesser. Chicago: Scott, Foresman, 1971.)

So here we have a psychologist finding what *is* among people he tested, and a philosopher thinking what *ought* to be. They seem to agree that the highest level is justice which comes from a man's own thinking. From a Christain view this is flawed. That is, it is not yet the highest value. Men can disagree on what justice is, and many of the troubles in our world arise from this disagreement. What seems to be omitted, from the Christian view, is the life of love. Omitted is the power of God to regenerate a person and enable him to live the highest kind of moral life. If our current high interest in developmental stages continues, we need Christian researchers to take up the challenge of researching our own specific Christian development. What might we find, for instance, at the upper levels if someone arranged the interview to reflect a more biblical approach and if some of the most mature Christians living today were interviewed? Kohlberg's research was conducted among a general population—including non-Christians—and this cannot be our ultimate guide in teaching morality. We have a better guide in the Bible.

Nevertheless, there is widespread interest among Christians in Kohlberg's theory, and in spite of its problems the research gives insight that can help us in teaching children. Most children of junior age are at Stages 1 and 2—the preconventional level. One fourth grade teacher proudly said of her class, "These children have a strong sense of fairness." She based this observation on numerous daily remarks such as these: "The boys had the ball last time; now it's our turn," "John didn't have to stay in when he was late, so why do I have to stay in?" Indeed, many teachers fall into the trap of trying to keep all the children happy under a "fairness" regime, thereby encouraging the children to continue to think at that level. And the more they think at that level the more complaints they have, so that teaching turns into a score-keeping job in an effort to keep things fair.

This concern for fairness, and the rigid application of rules is a Stage 2 kind of thinking. At this stage the child thinks the Golden Rule means, "He should treat me the way I treat him," if the treatment is good. If not, it may mean, "I should treat him the way he treats me." Perfect fairness.

When teachers understand the children's thinking they can learn not to respond at the same level. Instead of keeping score and aiming for perfect fairness, they can model and teach a slightly higher level. "God wants you to do good no matter what she does" (Stage 4, duty and respect for authority). "I'm proud of you for the way you acted just then" (Stage 3, approval of others). Kohlberg's research shows that children can understand the stages just one and two steps above where they are. This reasoning sounds good and right to them even though they haven't yet adopted it as their own. But reasoning more than two stages above the child's is not comprehended.

Thus a child at Stage 1 would not profit from the Stage 4 reasoning that it is his duty so submit to proper authority. These juniors—and most classes have them— are guided by punishment and reward. This they understand. On our learning model they are at Level 1 in discipline. Parents and teachers need to use punishment and reward to get them to act right. As they act right they will experience satisfaction in this and at times see how it satisfies others, too. By experience they come to the two-way thinking of "You be good to me and I'll be good to you." In this way they move from Stage 1 to Stage 2.

Each stage is like that. It leads into the next. Christain children do not escape these lower levels just because they have often heard how Jesus wants them to act. They need to work their way through the stages of growth one at a time.

In a church girls' club some 10-year-olds roleplayed

a situation where two girls treated a third one badly. Through several roleplays and intense discussions, the girls seemed to be learning much. "Boy, it really feels bad to be that girl." "I even felt bad treating her so mean." "Yeah, me too. I knew it was going to hurt her, but I just did it anyway." What does the Bible say about that? "Well, it tells us to love our enemies. She's not our enemy, but God wants us to love everybody." So how can you do that in school? "Well, in school we could think about the other girl's feelings. We could try to be friends with her." What if she isn't friendly to you? "Well, we could try. Anyway we don't have to be so mean."

And so it went. It sounded as if some of the girls were getting beyond Stage 2—the fairness stage of expecting friendliness back if they offer friendliness to another. Then a girl asked, "There are some kids at school that won't let me play hopscotch with them. How can I get them to let me play?" With this her Stage 2 thinking came through clearly. All the pious Bible talk aside, this girl wanted to make others treat her right. The teachers responded in this case with some Stage 4 guidance about how God wants her to act. She is responsible to God for herself. She can't make the other girls do right, but her good example may help them to learn.

Discussion and roleplay are good methods to use in helping children develop their moral reasoning. Through these, children can confront issues, practice thinking about them, and be exposed to higher levels of thinking. According to Kohlberg, children can attain the conventional level by about age 13. This corresponds to the age of beginning abstract operational thinking. In other words, a person must attain the higher intellectual level as defined by Piaget before he can reach this higher level of moral reasoning as defined by Kohlberg.

In moral reasoning a good many people remain at the conventional level—the law and order stages—for the rest of their lives, relatively few attaining the principled level. As with all the theories that have stages, we face the question about whether our job is to pull people up to higher stages. In America, especially, we are tempted to try to push everyone to a top level as soon as we have made some levels, and we ask how to do it faster and earlier. The rest of the world calls this the American question.

But is a person really better off if he reasons intellectually at a high stage? Or is he just as well off living in the law and order stage as long as he knows God's law? Whatever we may think is ideal, the fact is that many people live all their lives at the law and order stages, according to Kohlberg's research.

A common criticism of Kohlberg's system is that it centers around reasoning. Learning to reason at ever higher stages is supposed to lead a person eventually to high moral principles. But some point out that you can't reason about morals unless you know moral principles.

In Christian education we have always taught moral principles. And we have often added thinking, too. Now if we want to make use of Kohlberg's insight and work on moral reasoning, we can do this by teaching Bible principles at all stages. Children at Stage 1, punishment and reward orientation, have a natural understanding of Bible stories in which God punishes sin. Sometimes we tend to leave out those stories with young children, thinking they are not ready for them. But according to this theory it appears that primary and early junior years are the right time for them. Children in this stage readily understand God as authority and power. Heaven and hell as future reward and punishment are easily accepted into their thinking.

At Stage 2, children can accept a reasoning that they should act to please others and to please God. Juniors in this fairness stage can understand a two-way relationship. It seems fair to be nice to another and for that other person to be nice to you. Honesty is understood in this concrete way, of even exchanges, so that no one gets cheated. At this stage we can teach children to do good for God. God is the "other" in a two-way relationship with the child. God is good to him and he should be good for God. This helps overcome the reasoning of "He hit me so I get to hit him." It's not easy, though. It's a reasoning a Stage 1 child can begin to appreciate and grow toward.

While most junior children are at Stages 1 and 2, junior teachers who wish to work on moral reasoning should become familiar with the thinking of Stages 3 and 4. Then they can expose their children to these levels, as did the teachers in the girls' club example. As children see a better way, they eventually can come to think that way themselves.

Stage 3 is acting for the approval of others. In this stage, children of junior age can act for approval of parents and teachers and of God. There is opportunity yet during junior years for parents and teachers to do a lot of molding of the child. A child in teen years who is at Stage 3 gets much of his approval from peers, and if peers are exerting the wrong influence the teaching situation is very difficult. But juniors for the most part still want their approval from the significant adults in their lives. There are exceptions, of course.

Stage 4 is understanding the need for authority, rules, and order. The authority of parents, teachers, God, and the Bible all fit into this kind of thinking. Stage 4 thinking understands that it is good to respect these authorities. It sees duty and loyalty as good. There can be purpose beyond the self on which to base moral decisions. To help children see this kind of life is the great challenge of junior teachers in the area of moral reasoning.

We must remember, though, that reasoning is not the whole of it. Heart and conscience, as we have seen, are also important in moral development. We will see this described more fully in Chapter 6. Discipline builds conscience, and conscience is necessary to the child's moral development.

READING CHECK

1. Christian educators of the past have "missed the boat" on moral education because they didn't have our modern scientific knowledge.   T F

2. Conscience is when God talks to us.   T F

3. Conscience is the knowledge of God's law we have in our hearts.   T F

4. If we give children false teaching, their consciences become branded with error.   T F

5. If we fail to teach children right knowledge, their consciences become weak.   T F

6. Children need knowledge of love more than knowledge of rules about behavior.   T F

7. Bettelheim teaches that conscience is built by fear, which is instilled by discipline.   T F

8. We now know that this kind of fear is harmful to children.   T F

9. Kohlberg's theory describes stages in development of moral behavior.   T F

10. According to Kohlberg's research, most junior children consider consequences to themselves—punishment or satisfaction—rather than the expectations of society, authority, and so forth outside themselves.

T F

Answers: 1-F, 2-F, 3-T, 4-T, 5-T, 6-T, 7-T, 8-F, 9-F, 10-T

4 Development of Thinking

- *If you believe that inside the body there is a person, who has a mind, then you are not a behaviorist. The first part of this chapter points out some of the problems that arise when a Christian meets up with a behaviorist. Then it goes on to a somewhat better theory about thinking. You will find here a diagram and a description of the junior level of concrete thinking.*

We who believe in heart also believe in mind. That is important to say because there are some people who do not believe in mind, and they accuse us of seeing a "ghost in the machine." Who accuses you of that? It is the behaviorists.

If you haven't met behaviorism yet you will soon, because behaviorist thought, unfortunately, is having considerable influence on Christian education in our day. Just let it be known that you are against behavioral objectives and someone is sure to say to you, "Oh, but you believe it's important to teach behaviors to your children, don't you?" Of course you are concerned about behaviors. Sometimes. But you are concerned about the inner child much of the time, too. For every verse your friend can quote about *doing* the Word, you can quote one about *believing* or *knowing* or something else interior.

Your Christian friend who argues with you about

behavioral objectives is not really a behaviorist any more than you are. Christians cannot be. They cannot give up their belief in the person within the body. But your friend only wants to be in fashion educationally, so he is trying to use the fashionable idea of behavioral objectives and make it mean the same thing as "doing the Word." But it is not the same thing. "Doing the Word" implies first knowing it in the mind and loving it in the heart. Out of the heart of the child will come his actions. God judges by looking on the heart.

Now, the behaviorist says there is no mind or heart or other immaterial aspect of the person. None of this is reality. Only the sterile facts that can be validated scientifically by the senses are reality or truth. The "what is truth" question has been around since long before Pilate asked it, and behaviorists are only the more recent in a long line of people who deny mind as a way of knowing truth. One philosopher (a non-Christian) has said that there is no piece of nonsense that cannot gain the support of even the best trained minds, provided only that it is sanctioned by the current intellectual fashion.

Christian educators who are trying to be behaviorists must realize deep inside themselves that this system is nonsense. That is why they try so hard to adjust it in various ways to fit. Some say that you don't need a behavioral objective for every lesson, but you only need one for a unit. This doesn't get rid of the problem, but it does relieve it somewhat by pushing it farther off.

The basic problem is the overemphasis on behaviors. Imagine yourself as a student in a Bible class, and the teacher each week is analyzing you and deciding which behaviors he should change in you. He plans his lessons week by week to bring this change, that change, and another change. Some people have actually been in this situation, and they become so weighted down by it all that they drop out of the class. An individual must be free to think things over in his own mind and heart and to act with integrity from out of his own self.

Now imagine your class of juniors. Do you think you can "play God" with each child and decide on all the behavioral changes that you should bring about this year in your teaching?

This kind of emphasis on behaviors has come from a philosophy which believes there is no person, and all that exists is the body with its behaviors. You believe there is a person in each junior body in your class and you naturally treat them as persons, not as bodies. By your Christian common sense you know more about the children than behaviorists do. (In their science, that is. Even they handle their own children by common sense and not by science.) You even know more about teaching than they do, because teaching is a person-to-person affair and only people who believe in persons can see very clearly what teaching is all about.

The emphasis on behavioral objectives is bound to die out eventually in Christian education, if only because enthusiasm for them has already died out in secular education. They would die very quickly if everyone who talks about them would try to use them themselves.

So we put behaviorism behind us when we ask, "How do children think?" In the latter part of this chapter and in several later chapters we turn to other kinds of research for insights into children's thinking. But here, too, we need to keep in the back of our own minds that we are describing only parts of the child's thinking. Science cannot tell us really what mind is. It is still a mystery, and perhaps will be as long as we live in these bodies.

Mind is immaterial, as is heart. And the two are closely bound in Scripture. We see in the Bible that heart understands, meditates, knows and other functions that we tend to attribute to the head. (See Psalms 19:14; 49:3; Joshua 23:14.) Thoughts are born in the heart, both wise ones and wicked ones (Proverbs 6:18; Daniel 2:30).

A fourth grade class was talking about prayer and one highly intelligent boy asked, "How can we talk to God? He's way up there and . . ." Sara, a retarded girl, broke in, and with gestures and emphatic tones said, "It's easy! You just tell Him what you want and He hears you right here."

Sara obviously understands more about prayer than many Ph.D.s. There is much more to mind than we see when we measure intelligence and talk about concrete and abstract thinking and similar matters. So all the time we study mental development we must keep our common sense about us. We can't throw common sense aside and make it our whole goal to help children move from concrete thinking to abstract thinking any more than we make it our whole goal to change behaviors. Let your goals come out of the Bible and out of your Christian beliefs, and let the study of children's thinking help you where it will.

We will look now at a very influential current theory of mental development. This comes from the work of Jean Piaget in Switzerland. Piaget has given us a system of age levels and stages and numerous detailed descriptions of children's thinking.

The diagram in Figure 2 shows three major stages and how the children in those stages think about a particular stick problem. The youngest child here is in the preoperational stage. If you show him the red and blue sticks and ask which is longer, he can see that the blue is longer and give you the correct answer. Now if you hide the red stick and bring out the green one, something interesting happens. Ask if the green one is longer than the red and you have given the child a problem he must do in his head, since the red stick is no longer in view. A child at the preoperational stage can't do problems in his head. If you put everything out on the table he can solve the problem by looking at the sticks. But you have hidden the red stick, so the child says something like,

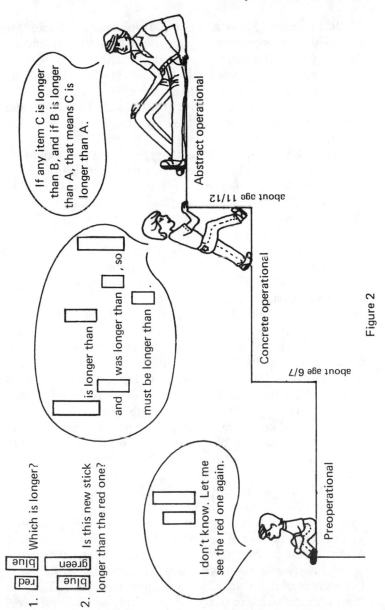

Figure 2

"I don't know. Show me the red one again." This stage is called "preoperational," meaning that these children cannot yet do this kind of mental operation.

Now, most of your juniors are at the next stage. They can do concrete operations. That is, they can think in their heads about the sticks, including the hidden one, and they can tell you that the green stick is longer.

The third stage in the diagram is called "abstract operations." The child here doesn't have to think about one concrete set of sticks. He can understand that in any case like this the third stick would be longer than the first. He can even go beyond the ideas of length and of sticks and understand the general proposition that if C is greater than B, and B is greater than A, then C is greater than A. This is abstract thinking.

In the later junior years some children can begin to think abstractly about some things. But for the most part we should get used to the idea that our junior children are thinking concretely. They think about a specific, actual situation and do not generalize about other possible situations.

What does this mean for Bible teaching? That is a good question, and one we can only make some guesses about at the present time. Piaget's research, and most other research of this type, concerns logical thinking in matters of physics or mathematics. Only a few studies, such as those described in the next chapter, concern stories or other kinds of content that are closer to what we are doing in Christian education.

Probably the main thing we should do is try to teach about specific happenings and specific examples as much as possible. These are concrete. It is amazing how much of the Bible is concrete. Jesus said if someone strikes us on one cheek we should turn and let him strike us on the other, also. Our adult reaction too often is, "He didn't literally mean that." We decide it is figurative, and then we try to think up the kinds of situations where we might in a figurative way turn the other cheek. But our examples are not more true than the original example. Children can easily learn the original example and they have no trouble understanding what it means. Younger children have a good Bible lesson if that's all they learn. Older children can think of examples from their lives, not so as to dilute the Bible example but just to give it a wider application. Again, if that's all they do, if they stay on this level of specific, concrete thinking, they have a good Bible lesson. The abstract idea of turning the other cheek as a principle by which to live can come later—if it needs to come at all.

Jesus said to love your neighbor. Then He told the story about the Samaritan. Much of His teaching was in the form of specific examples. Old Testament history is not full of generalizations and summaries as so many history books are. But we know the Jews by knowing Abraham, Joshua, David and others. We know each of these people not by summaries, such as "He conquered the land," but by stories—Joshua marching around Jericho or praying for the sun to stand still.

When we're using Bible stories to teach, we will do better to decide where the specific story begins and start from there. An opening paragraph that packs in lots of background information calls for too much "mental operating" on the part of the children, so it doesn't clarify the teaching for them. It muddies it, instead. A bad example of this technique might read like this. "Today we have a story about Miriam who was Moses' sister, and you remember how she helped watch baby Moses in the basket before they crossed the Red Sea when Pharoah kept all the Israelites as slaves in Egypt and all the baby boys were supposed to be killed." A little exaggerated, maybe, but you can see the mental operations we ask for when we try too hard to connect things for the children. We do, of course, want the Bible to be more than a jumble of stories in children's minds. We want them to connect their learnings, and techniques for doing this are given in Chapter 8. An opening story paragraph is not the best place for this.

An aspect of stories that makes them easy to understand is sometimes called "human meaning." Human meaning in stories comes through to children in ways we haven't analyzed yet. While researchers are busy trying to determine what logic children understand from various teachings, children go right on in their own ways getting all kinds of meaning that we don't know how to measure. So, while we can glean some hints from this kind of research about how to teach Bible content, we really don't have a full formula.

One technique that seems not helpful is the use of symbols such as a triangle for the Trinity. Symbols do not achieve concreteness. The more symbolic something is, the more abstract it is. On the diagram (Figure 2) the first child must use the sticks to solve the problem. He could not do it at all if you simply told him about the sticks in words. The second child may be able to do the problem if you explain it in words (symbols), but the words, for him, are tied very closely with sticks which he images in his head. The third child can do without the image of objects and can operate with words only, or even with mathematical symbols: If $C > B$ and $B > A$, then $C > A$. Mathematicians can operate with symbols only, that have no connection with objects.

The object is concrete. Words are a step away, but they can still be tied to concrete objects. Symbols are more steps away. It takes a high level of abstract thinking to get any meaning from symbols. So a circle symbol does not help children understand what God is like, and a triangle does not help them understand the Trinity. Children do learn to verbalize answers for us about these symbols, but their real thinking is another matter.

Learning to think abstractly, to reason about the

possible and not only the actual, seems to be largely a result of education, or of social, cooperative activities. The Soviet psychologist A. R. Luria conducted research in 1931-32 among illiterate, unschooled, nomadic people who were brought from remote areas into cooperatives. For political reasons this research was not published until 1974. Here are two excerpts from interviews of adults still in a concrete stage, unable to reason in their heads. (From *Cognitive Development: Its Cultural and Social Foundations.* Cambridge: Harvard University Press, pages 108 and 112.)

> Cotton can only grow where it is hot and dry. In England it is cold and damp. Can cotton grow there? "I don't know." Think about it. "I've only been in the Kashgar country; I don't know beyond that . . ." But on the basis of what I said to you, can cotton grow there? "If the land is good, cotton will grow there, but if it is damp and poor, it won't grow. If it's like the Kashgar country, it will grow there too. If the soil is loose, it can grow there too, of course."

The original syllogism is repeated and the interviewer asks again:

> What can you conclude from my words? "If it's cold there, it won't grow; if the soil is loose and good, it will." But what do my words suggest? "Well, we Moslems, we Kashgars, we're ignorant people; we've never been anywhere, so we don't know if it's hot or cold there."

In another syllogism the interviewer explained that in the North where there is snow all bears are white. Novaya Zemlya is in the Far North and there is always snow there. He asked, then, what color the bears are in the North.

"You've seen them, you know. I haven't seen them, so how could I say?!" But on the basis of what I said, what do you think? "But I never saw them, so how could I say?!"

These unschooled people were unable to categorize objects into classes such as tools, cooking utensils, or plants. Names for groups of objects like that come from schooling, or at least from social interaction. Individuals who have no need for such categories seem not to develop them. Try looking around the room where you are now and seeing some of the geometrical shapes—rectangles, circles, cylinders and so forth. Now imagine that you have never been taught the word "shape" or the term "geometrical shape." Do you think you would ever have come to lump the lampshade shape, the ceiling shape, and others together in a category? And would you further have developed general rules and principles for finding their areas and perimeters and volumes? Most of such naming of abstractions and thinking about, or operating on, abstractions comes from learning from other people. You will extend people's thinking and knowledge a bit when you invent some new useful category. When you teach your children a category and a name for it—such as *patriarchs*—you provide them a new tool to think with.

Now, our children begin their junior years thinking largely on the concrete level, and they end them thinking at least in some matters on an abstract level. So we need a two-pronged approach in our teaching. We should keep much of our teaching at a concrete level, so the children can understand us, but at the same time we should work at building the meaning of abstract concepts so they can come to understand and use these.

Figure 3 shows three ladders of abstraction. At the bottom of the Samuel ladder we find a concrete act that Samuel performed. He opened the temple doors in the

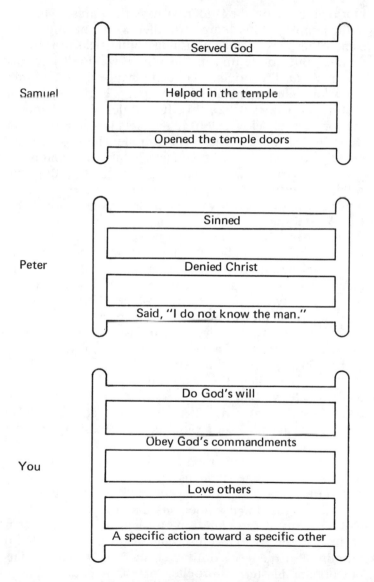

Samuel

- Served God
- Helped in the temple
- Opened the temple doors

Peter

- Sinned
- Denied Christ
- Said, "I do not know the man."

You

- Do God's will
- Obey God's commandments
- Love others
- A specific action toward a specific other

Figure 3

morning. Next on the ladder we have the phrase, "helped in the temple." This lumps together with opening doors some other acts such as polishing candlesticks or running errands. But notice that in this phrase we don't know as much about the original concrete happening. We only know one characteristic of it—helping. Each step on an abstraction ladder is like this. It includes all the happenings or objects below it, but it abstracts less and less from them as we move higher. The top step here is "served God." This includes all of Samuel's helping acts and more yet—his praying or worshiping acts, for instance. But now we know even less about the original concrete act. We don't know that it was in the temple, or that it was helpful. We only know that it in some way served God. The Peter ladder and the You ladder work similarly.

We adults can talk easily about serving God and doing God's will because we have wide backgrounds of specific instances to give meaning to these terms. It would tire us to always stay down on the concrete level. To do this we would have to include whole lists of specific instances to say what we mean, so we find it easier to chunk many instances together, to categorize them in an abstract term. The Kashgars, presumably, would have had to say, "Bring the shovel, the hoe, the rake, and the spade too." They had no category name to say, "Bring me the tools." We adults not only have names for our abstractions, we also are able to move them around in our heads—operate on them mentally.

But junior children are not good at that yet. When we want them to understand us well, we will stay close to the bottom of the ladder practically all the time for younger children and a good share of the time for older children. But at the same time we will be teaching them abstract terms. We will in many ways be building up meanings for the terms on these ladders, as well as numerous other Bible terms—prophet, patriarch, church, atonement, miracle, gospel, disciple, parable, law, grace, glory, spiritual, kingdom of God, and others.

A name for an object—a yo-yo, for instance—might at times be learned and remembered on one hearing, but not so with abstract words. All of us, even adults, need to meet a word many times in many contexts before it becomes part of our usable vocabulary. Once a teacher grasps this fact, he or she can better teach some of the numerous Bible concepts that juniors need to learn.

The following chapter continues the topic of children's thinking, looking specifically at metaphor and analogy. Since the Bible is full of this kind of writing it is important for us to try to understand children's metaphorical thinking.

READING CHECK

1. Behaviorists do not believe in mind as an immaterial part of man.   T F

2. According to Piaget's theory, most junior children are in the concrete operational stage of thinking.   T F

3. In the stick problem, "concrete operational" means that the child needs all the sticks out on the table in order to solve the problem.   T F

4. Symbol drawings help make your teaching concrete.   T F

5. Children can be learning about some abstract concepts even while they are in the concrete operational stage.   T F

6. If you call Abraham a *patriarch,* children are likely to have a better understanding of Abraham's place as a father of the Jewish people.   T F

7. If you explain why Abraham is called a *patriarch,* you are beginning to build children's understanding of that abstract word.   T F

Answers: 1—T, 2—T, 3—F, 4—F, 5—T, 6—F, 7—T

5 Understanding Metaphor

● *If the last chapter didn't get you hooked yet on the study of children's thinking, try this one. Here you will have an inside look at two research studies. On the first study you will see some of the questions used and you can analyze the results in the way a researcher does. On the second study you can do the analyzing again (it's not hard), and then you can hear the children's own voices as they answered questions in the interviews.*

Metaphor is so built into our language that most of the time we don't even notice it. John the Baptist came to prepare the *way* of the Lord, to make straight in the *desert* a *highway* for our God, to make His *paths straight.* What kind of desert did John's highway cut through, and how did he make it straight? All these words are metaphors. If you try rewriting the verses about John to eliminate the metaphors in them you are likely to fall into using still other metaphors. You might mention the *darkness* of the world, the *light* of God, *turning* men, or *pointing* them to Jesus.

Our language is so full of metaphors that many of them are now "dead," and we no longer call them metaphors. We reserve the title for unusual poetic uses: "The fog comes on little cat feet." Thinking of an unusual metaphor is a creative act.

There is something profound and basic in metaphoric language. Some theoreticians see this as the way language develops. Kathy Lynn Hutson has proposed that after God gave the basic categories in the beginning, all language developed metaphorically from these ("Metaphor: An Evidence from Design of the Creation Model" in *Creation Social Science and Humanities Quarterly,* Volume 1, Numbers 1 and 2). God spoke creation into being. He said, "Let there be light," and there was light. The word came before the thing. God also named things after they were organized. When light and darkness were separated He called them Day and Night. When land and water were separated He called them Earth and Seas. Later He let Adam continue the task of "calling" or "naming" things. Here is a theory of the origin of language. If our words continued metaphorically the true categories from the pure language of God, our knowledge of the real nature of things would be closer to truth. But sin and decay have distorted and confused this process.

Regardless of how language began, it is evident now that metaphor is indeed basic to our thinking and understanding. Metaphor, analogy and parables are all based on the idea of likenesses between things. Bible literature is full of these and we will consider them together in this chapter.

In some respects 9-year-old children are quite close to adult level in understanding metaphor. Each year the massive National Assessment program tests large numbers of people in the United States. In the literature test one section aims to test understanding of metaphoric language. On six items one year the 9-year-olds' correct answers ranged from 47 to 91 percent. On these same items adults ranged from 59 to 95 percent. This is not as large a difference as one might at first expect. And we can profit from examining the types of metaphors used in the items. Some items each year are not released to the public because they are used for the next retesting, along with new items. Unfortunately, three extremes here are on unreleased items—that is, the children's high score of 91 and the adults' high score of 95, and their low score of 59 percent. What kind of item was it where nine out of ten children answered correctly? It would be interesting to know. Analyzing the four released items gives us some good ideas about what is easy for children and what is more difficult. Figure 4 shows two poems used and the questions based on each. At the left are the percentages of 9-year-olds and adults who got each item correct.

Of these four items the most difficult for 9-year-olds is Item 1. Only about half the 9-year-olds got this one. Here two nouns are equated: *Hope* is a *bird*. In biblical content this is similar to understanding in Jesus' story of the two houses that *house* equals *life*, or that *rock* means *truth* or *Jesus' sayings*, or that *sand* means *falsehood*.

Items 2 and 4 are stated as adjectives. Hope is cheerful and fog is quiet. These items are easier, as quite a few more children got these. Item 3 asks children to equate cat's feet and mist (fog). These are nouns again, but if we look for a reason why it is easier than the other noun item, we perhaps find it in the fact that the item called it "slow-moving mist." In other words, action was included.

Missing in all of these is out-and-out action: The potter smashes and builds again; God smashes and builds again. But the items that get closer to action are easier. Here is a list in order of most difficult to least difficult. (Emphasis added in the quotations below.)

Hope is made to be like *a bird.*   47.3%

The cat's feet are compared to
slow moving mist.   63.4%

The fog is meant to be seen as
quiet and stealthy.   70.3%

Hope is a thing with feathers
That perches in the soul,
And sings the tune without the words,
And never stops at all.
(Emily Dickinson)

Age 9	Adult	
		1. Hope is made to be like
47.3	76.5	a bird.
		the soul.
		an Indian.
		I don't know.

2. Hope is meant to be
   silent and shy.
   irregular and sad.

75.5	81.0	cheerful and dependable.
		I don't know.

The fog comes
on little cat feet.

It sits looking
over harbor and city
on silent haunches
and then moves on.
(Carl Sandburg)

3. The cat's feet are compared to
   the rain.

63.4	85.2	slow moving mist.
		the tops of buildings.
		I don't know.

4. The fog is meant to be seen as
   loud and clumsy.
   majestic and proud.

70.3	89.7	quiet and stealthy.
		I don't know.

Figure 4

Hope is meant to be *cheerful
and dependable.*   75.5%

From this, it appears that it really would not be difficult to teach Emily Dickinson's poem to juniors. All it would take is a story, or picture and conversation, about a bird perching in a tree, singing a happy tune, on and on and on. Or better yet, observe a live, singing bird. Then suggest the thought that hope perches inside us and sings a happy tune, too. We might try thinking of examples like hoping for a happy surprise on a birthday, hoping for heaven, and so forth, and then read again Dickinson's beautiful lines and see how full of meaning they are. We could test the children this way.

Hope is meant to
    ____ be soft like feathers.
    ____ be invisible like the soul.
    ____ sing like a bird.
    ____ I don't know.

Ninety percent or more of juniors should get this item. The vivid action of singing reaches more juniors than any of the likenesses in the National Assessment questions. Of course, it could be seen as an incomplete translation of the metaphor. But what does hope *do* in this poem? The other test items say it *is* like a bird or it *is* cheerful. We might say it *makes* us happy. All these verbs lack action. If you had Adam's job of naming things, what would you call the action of hope? What would you say hope does? Emily Dickinson said it sings. Is there a better word?

The key to using metaphor with young children is to dwell on action whenever possible. The shepherd protects; Jesus protects. The potter can smash when he wants; God can smash when He wants. The potter makes it better; God makes it better. This close union of shepherd and

Jesus, or bird and hope, is the way an artist thinks. Young children think like artists. Psychologists have recognized this, and educational studies of children's understanding of literature or poetry have shown it. In Piaget's scheme of things, it would be called transduction—not induction or deduction, but transduction—moving across from one item to the other. It is not truly a reasoning by analogy, but it is its beginning. This transductive beginning of understanding analogy is found in primary children, and by junior ages it has grown into a true reasoning from analogy.

Analogy can be diagramed as in Figure 5. Dickinson's poem put onto the drawing would be something like Figure 6. Other likenesses could also be put in the circle. For instance, hope perches. That is more appropriate than tramping or slithering would have been. It has feathers. That's more delightful than thorns or hoofs. And it sings continuously. That's more hopeful than a quick burst of song that dies away into silence. So there are many ways hope is like a bird. But for simplicity we have used the most active one, which is the most important anyway.

This study of analogy is important for teachers because analogy is basic to our language. And language is basic to our thinking. Thinking is dependent upon language in such fundamental ways that some scientists believe characteristics of our language shape our thinking. So what does metaphor or analogy in language tell us about thinking?

In the 1930s psychologist Charles Spearman had something to say about this. He proposed three "principles" of thinking which correspond to the three parts of the analogy diagram we are using here (*Creative Mind*. New York: Appleton, 1931). Spearman's principles of thinking are similar to certain parts of more recent theory, and in particular the three-level theory set forth in this book. These simple diagrams make beautifully

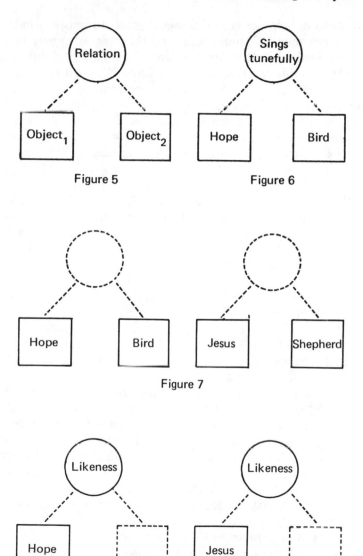

Figure 5

Figure 6

Figure 7

Figure 8

clear to us some complex things that we do in our minds.

Spearman's first principle of thinking is experience. To understand the hope poem, for instance, children need experience of hope and of birds. Without this, they can go no further. They need experiences as thinking material. Experiences are the objects or subjects to think about. This is information learning, or Level 1 on our learning model in the next chapter.

Now, having experiences, a higher kind of thinking is to relate them. In the case we are considering, the relation is a likeness—both sing. To diagram this thinking process we leave the circle blank (Figure 7). If the child figures out the missing part, if he sees how the two objects or persons are alike, he is thinking on Level 2, seeing relationships, conceptualizing. We do this when we understand Dickinson's poem or Jesus' teaching about the shepherd.

A third and more difficult kind of thinking is diagramed in Figure 8. To think of a correlate, something that is like hope, is a higher mental act. It is more difficult than either of the earlier examples. It has often been called the creative act. Scientists do this when they conceive of the structure of a chemical substance. Novelists do it when they conceive a novel to make a statement about life. People as different as psychologists and mathematicians have come by different routes to the conclusion that educing a correlate is at the heart of much mental creativity. Dickinson put *bird* in the blank box in Figure 8. You can try to put something else there, and see what is involved in the creative act.

In summary, Spearman's three kinds of thinking involve:

1. The principle of experience.
2. The principle of relationships.
3. The principle of correlates.

These three kinds of thinking correspond to the three levels of our learning model—the informational, the conceptual, and the creative. The third, creative, principle has been called other names by other people. Arthur Koestler called it "bisociation" (*Insight and Outlook.* New York: MacMillan, 1949). He saw the bisociative act to be at the basis not only of good poetry, but of good humor and of inventions and discoveries.

It is well to remember that the experience (or information) level is absolutely necessary for the higher levels. Much emotional zeal is spent on discovery learning (Level 2) and on creativity (Level 3). People try to do these in a sort of pure form, ignoring the fact that to think we must first have some things to think about, or the fact that to create we must create from something.

These three thinking processes are not tied to ages, as are the stages in the Piaget system. People of any age can perform all the processes. For instance, preschool children can 1) string beads, 2) conceptualize bead patterns, and 3) create new patterns. Junior children can 1) collect facts about Bible characters, 2) relate the facts on charts or graphs, and 3) create new ideas for charts or graphs. Mathematicians can go through these steps with formulas. Perhaps you noticed that the Piaget developmental levels are implicit in the choice of examples above. The preschooler performs his thinking on actual objects, the junior child performs his thinking on concrete characters and charts (which can begin to contain simple abstractions), and the mathematician thinks his with abstract symbols.

For another view of children's understanding of analogies we can use the Piaget approach and examine what happens across ages. A study on understanding parables has shown that children of ages 9, 10, and 11 grow rapidly in this ability (Beechick, *Children's Understanding of Parables.* Ann Arbor, Mich.: University Microfilms, 1974, No. 73-14277). Twelve-year-olds were not included in the study because they are "off the scale," so to speak. They have fairly well mastered the skills tested.

Three stories were used in this study. We will take space here to report only one story—The Potter. The children were given this story, which they read aloud and then were interviewed on.

God said to Jeremiah, "Go to the potter's house. I will tell you something there." So Jeremiah went to the potter's house.

The potter was making a pot of clay. The pot was not turning out good, so the potter smashed the clay into a ball. Then he started again to make another pot from the clay.

God said to Jeremiah, "See, I can do like that with the nations. I can smash them or build them up again."

What does God want us to learn from this story?

The interviews were transcribed and studied in various ways to rate the children according to these three stages.

1. The child can only repeat facts or elements of the story, or concrete elements from outside the story.

2. The child can make an application in a simple way, such as be kind, obey God, and so forth.

3. The child can understand an analogy in an abstract way, relating in some way the situation in the story with a life situation; he sees an appropriate spiritual meaning.

For those interested in Piaget's theory, these stages correspond roughly as follows. Stage 1 is Piaget's preoperational stage. Most junior children are beyond this. Stage 2 is definitely in the concrete operational stage. Most junior children are here. Stage 3 is not so clear-cut. It seems to be borderline between concrete operational and abstract operational. The children compare a concrete story with an abstract meaning. Many older junior children could do this well. They were not tested otherwise to see if they would rate as being abstract operational. Probably some of them would not.

Figure 9 shows how junior children scored on understanding parables. This shows that practically all juniors are at Stage 2 or above. Only a very few of the youngest ones are on Stage 1. It shows also a tremendous growth across the ages. At age 9, 10 percent of the children understood the parable abstractly. At age 10 this has grown to 31 percent and at age 11 to 79 percent. Presumably age 12 would be practically 100 percent. Combining figures to see how many children are at Stage 2 or above, we also see a picture of good growth through junior years. Sixty-nine percent of 9-year-olds are at or above Stage 2. This grows to 81 percent by age 10 and 99 percent by age 11.

Figure 10 shows a different picture. This is the percentage of children who understood the analogies within the story itself. This shows how junior children do on the second level of thinking for this particular story. How do they conceptualize or understand the analogy of two objects? According to this they do surprisingly well. Some growth is shown here between 9- and 11-year-olds. But since the 9s are halfway there already, there is not a great deal of room for advancement. And these analogies are all of the noun type, which we saw earlier is the most difficult. If we had scores here for the "smashing" analogies they undoubtedly would be higher yet. The full study, which included two other stories and children younger than age 9, showed this:

age	Stage 1	Stage 2	Stage 3	Stage 2 or above
11	1%	20%	79%	99%
10	19%	50%	31%	81%
9	31%	59%	10%	69%

Figure 9

age	potter = God	clay = nations (stated)	clay = you (inferred)
11	90%	80%	70%
10	70%	50%	60%
9	60%	40%	60%

Figure 10

1. Analogies of "actions" are understood first. (Smashing and building up.)

2. Analogies of "actors" are understood next. (Potter, God.)

3. Analogies of "objects acted upon" are understood last. (Clay, nations, you.)

All of these are easier if the child himself is one of the pair: the child is the clay, or the sheep.

So you can taste a little of the flavor of children's thinking, we will quote here some of the children's comments on the potter story. None of these children remembered ever hearing this story before. A few had heard of the idea, probably from the hymn line which says, "Thou art the Potter, I am the clay." Interestingly enough, the results on this story were similar to those on the story of the two houses, which all the children knew previously. This shows that the ratings here are truly ratings of thinking levels, and not of learned or remembered material.

Stage 1 Children. These children often commented on the smashing. This vivid word impressed almost all. "He can smash the world." "No one can smash Him." "He can smash the nations and build them up again." Darrell, 9, learned "not to be foolish and smash the clay." His word *foolish* was likely suggested by the previous conversation on the story of the two houses.

Occasionally a child showed some surprising insights. Jim, 9, was asked if he saw something in the story like himself. " 'Cause someone made me. God made me." So what part in the story is like you? "We are made out of dirt." So are you like the potter, or the clay, or . . . ? (No answer.) Jim also saw something like God. "No one can smash Him." This unique arrangement of ideas apparently satisfied him.

Stage 2 Children. When Jack, 11, was asked what in the story is most like God, he answered, "When he smashes the clay." After some discussion the same question was repeated and he said, "Jeremiah when he smashes it." Later the question was reversed: You say the clay is like the nations; now what is the potter like? "A builder." What kind? "A clay builder, pot builder." Jack could see the analogy to God in the action, but he could not see it in the nouns.

George, 9, is another example of this. When asked what in the story is like God he answered, "Oh, whenever he thought that his pot was looking bad he'd smash it." Do you see anything in the story that's like you? "Yeah, in some ways." What might be like you? "Sometimes I'll step on something." Do you see anything in there that's like your nation? "That He can destroy it." You mean God could destroy it? "Yes." Is there anything in the story of the potter that would be like the nation? "That he destroys his pot when it don't look good."

Karen, 9, also used the word "smash" when first asked what was like God. A brief conversation about smashing ensued. Then she was pressed to look for something in the story that was like God, and finally said she saw something. What? "The *potter*, because *he makes pottery* and *God made us* and He could smash it." (Emphasis added.) Even after making such a clear statement of the analogy she could not name what in the story was like us. When given the choice of potter, pot, and clay and asked which was like her, she answered, "None." Likewise, she could find no analogy for nations. And she even omitted her own clearly stated analogy for God and returned to her original idea of smashing when she was asked later in the interview what God wants us to learn from the story. She answered, "He wants us to learn that He can smash us and He can build us up again."

These Stage 2 children often used the word "when" in response to a question of "what" is like God or "what" is like you. Dave, 10: "When I do bad, like I turned out bad and then I asked the Lord to be saved and He smashes it up and throws it away and then I don't have that sin in my heart anymore." Jolene, 10: "When that guy smashed the clay and started to make another pot." Jerry, 10, had this surprising analogy: "When He was crucified He rose again after He was put in the grave."

Lessons that these children learned from the story included, "That He rules the earth," "That God can make you over again when you're saved," "That if we're a sinner and we don't, and we failed, He would bring us up again," and "Well, if you don't live a Christian life maybe He won't use you."

Stage 3 Children. Jean, 11, said God wants us to learn "That He has complete rule over the world." Art, 10: "He forms us from the clay and uses us to be the person He wants us to be." Eddie, 11: "Before I was saved I wasn't turning out good." And then? "Jesus saved me." And then after that? "He made me better." Janice, 10: "I think He wants us to learn that we should obey Him and we should do right and if we don't obey Him He can just, you know, sort of ruin us, and then if we want to be built up again in Jesus He can build us up."

Janice hedged just a little when she realized her analogy was leading her to say that something might break in God's hands. Roy, 11, had great difficulty on this point. Roy said he was like the clay "Because . . . I know, except I don't know the words very well. Like God could build us up into a good Christian or . . . " Or? "Or He could . . . He wouldn't make you . . . He wouldn't want you to be a bad Christian. Oh, I don't know how to explain that part." You're trying to figure out what would happen if somebody was a bad Christian? "Uh huh." What did the potter do when the pot wasn't turning out good? "He smashed it—started to make another one." What do you think God's trying to tell us with that? "That if you've been living a real bad life that you can get saved, or even if you're a Christian and you're living a real bad life that He can change you into a new person."

Getting inside children's thinking is fascinating for teachers. The more of this we do the better we understand them and the better we can teach them. Concerning metaphoric language, the Bible is full of it. As for metaphoric thinking, junior children can handle it quite well. Bible metaphors are a way of making abstract meanings concrete, so our younger children can think of them concretely and our older children can grow in understanding them abstractly. They all can gain some meaning. Metaphors, parables and analogies are rich in meaning.

READING CHECK

1. Metaphoric language is a fancy kind of language we reserve for poems and flowery literature.   T F

2. Children understand analogies with action earlier than they understand analogies of nouns.   T F

3. In the story of the lost sheep more children are likely to understand that they are lost than that they are sheep.   T F

Emily Dickinson invented the idea that a bird is like hope, and when we read her poem we understand the likeness between bird and hope.

4. Dickinson's thinking was at Level 3.   T F
5. Our thinking in this is at Level 2.   T F
6. Juniors cannot do this Level 2 thinking.   T F

7. Children of any age can think creatively.   T F
8. Children of any age can think abstractly.   T F

Answers: 1–F, 2–T, 3–T, 4–T, 5–T, 6–F, 7–T, 8–F

6 A Model of Learning

• *We start the second half of this book with a Christian theory of learning. Your Bible-believing heart should find this theory more satisfying than others you have read about.*

The great teacher Moses neared the end of his life and gave his last instructions to his people. He reminded them of what they had seen and learned, and told them to teach future generations. "Only take heed to thyself, and keep thy soul diligently, lest thou forget the things which thine eyes have seen, and lest they depart from thy heart all the days of thy life: but teach them thy sons, and thy sons' sons" (Deuteronomy 4:9).

Over three thousand years later people are still teaching the law of God to their sons and their sons' sons. How were the teachers to prepare? Go to methods school? Bone up on theory? No, they were to diligently keep their own souls and hearts. The souls and hearts of the children would learn from the souls and hearts of the parents. Moses speaks throughout the rest of the book of Deuteronomy, giving the content of the teaching, but he says almost nothing about the method. He tells the people what to teach, but not how. Where he does touch on the how, he mostly is admonishing the people to keep everlastingly at it.

Hear, O Israel: The Lord our God is one Lord: And thou shalt love the Lord thy God with all thine heart, and with all thy soul, and

> with all thy might. And these words, which I command thee this
> day, shall be in thine heart: And thou shalt teach them diligently
> unto thy children, and shalt talk of them when thou sittest in
> thine house, and when thou walkest by the way, and when thou
> liest down, and when thou risest up. And thou shalt bind them
> for a sign upon thine hand, and they shall be as frontlets be-
> tween thine eyes. And thou shalt write them upon the posts of
> thy house, and on thy gates (Deuteronomy 6:4-7).

The teaching methods of Jesus have been the subject of numerous books and other writings. A few of these writings are good, but some merely succeed in finding in Jesus some modern theory the writer is trying to support. In the 1920s a writer could find that Jesus used the "project" method (sending the disciples out to preach). Only a theological liberal could do this at that time because projects were associated with Deweyism, and Deweyism was a dirty word to conservatives in those days. But by the 70s conservatives could find "activities," as no one connected them with Deweyism anymore. In the 40s many people were writing that Jesus used visuals (lilies, temple), and the use of flannelgraph spread widely. In the 70s the writings began to say that Jesus' real method was "modeling." Whatever the passing fashion might be, a writer can find that it's just what Jesus did.

Mind reading accompanied many of these analyses: Jesus knew that people remember more of what they see, so He pointed to the lilies; Jesus felt they were ready now for the next step in learning; Jesus' next question was designed to accomplish such and such. These mind-reading exercises, of course, only help us to read the writers' minds and not the mind of Jesus.

An honest analysis of Jesus' teaching methods has to recognize that in most incidents that can in our usual sense be called teaching situations Jesus "opened his mouth and taught them, saying . . . " or "he expounded unto them in all the Scriptures the things concerning himself." It's surprising how many studies miss the proper proportion of these. One suspects that the writers are afraid of appearing to promote the lecture method.

It just may be that our century places too much emphasis on method. The 1920s was a period of excitement and innovations in teaching methods in Christian education, but by the 30s had come disappointment with the results. Some felt that the problem might have come from sacrificing essential Bible teaching to the new methods. The 60s, in public education, was another decade of experimenting and innovating. This hit the churches in full force in the 70s, and by the 80s some were asking again the question of the 30s: Have we sacrificed too much of Bible content?

Moses used much time in his life's closing speeches to tell the people what to teach their sons and sons' sons. Jesus told His disciples to teach all nations to observe "all things" that He has commanded. Paul entrusted his teachings to Timothy and told him to pass them on to other faithful men who in turn would pass them on to still others—the Moses system still working.

All these teachers of teachers, clearly and at great length, told the teachers what to teach. We can't miss that emphasis. For the methods we pull out hints from here and there and make what we want of them.

This does not seem strange if we hold a biblical view of the human heart and soul and mind. Our minds are conscious of self. We know we are living persons, living souls. The heart knows itself. A heart that has learned doesn't need anyone to tell it what learning is; the father knows how to teach his son. Methods may be as broad as East and West, they may be as different as the twelfth century and the twenty-first century, but the Christian view of learning can incorporate most of them.

We have pointed out thus far three criteria for a Christian theory of learning: 1) It must hold heart in an important place, 2) it must emphasize content as well as development and methods, and 3) it can allow for great flexibility in teaching methods. We add a fourth. 4) It should incorporate scientific knowledge as far as that seems consistent with biblical views.

The model proposed here is intended to fit this description. The basic form of the model (Figure 11) is taken from Wilson, Robeck, and Michael (*Psychological Foundations of Learning.* New York: McGraw-Hill, 1969). That is, the three levels representing three kinds of thinking, the two sides representing the cognitive aspect and the motivational aspect, and the culminating merging of these two, are from the Wilson-Robeck model, but the labels and ideas represented by the various circles and arrows have been changed so much that these educational psychologists cannot be held responsible for what appears here.

We will now look briefly at each part of the model. Then in following chapters, we will explore more thoroughly certain aspects of it.

Information Learning. To begin at the bottom left of the model, we find the level of information learning. This is sheer knowing the stuff: Samuel helped Eli in the temple, Moses led the Israelites, Jesus is the Son of God, Genesis is the first book of the Bible, and so forth. What is often called rote learning is included in this circle, the kind of learning that is obtained more mechanically than thinkingly. If we were to incorporate behaviorist theory into this model it would belong mostly at this level. Any learning by conditioning is here, also repetition, memorizing, and all the learning of bits and pieces and larger chunks of information that children learn without experiencing a higher level of thinking. This is Level 1 thinking. This level is not less important or of less value than the higher levels. Actually, it is necessary, and cannot be neglected in efforts to reach higher levels of thinking. It provides the material for thinking at the higher levels.

Conceptual Learning. At this level the child sees

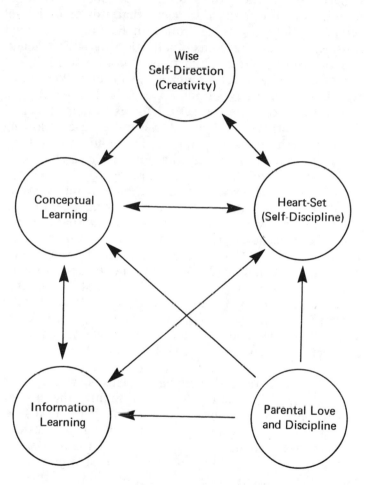

Figure 11

meaningful relationships among facts. It is the "aha" experience. We do not shorten this label to *concept learning* because it must be clear that this second level refers to the *process* of conceptualization. The child must experience the conceptualization, not the teacher. It is not simply that a child thinks about a small "fact" at Level 1 and a larger "concept" at Level 2. We do not feed him facts at Level 1 and concepts at Level 2. But we can organize content and set up things to help the child do more learning on Level 2. Several of the following chapters in this book are concerned with how to do this.

The arrow between information learning and conceptual learning points in both directions. The upward direction is to show that it takes a base of information, it takes facts, for the mind to experience conceptualization. The downward direction is to indicate that the concept then reaches out for more facts to fill it. Some reader may say, "Aha, I see the difference between Level 1 and Level 2 thinking." Then in his next class session he will notice various happenings or remarks of the children that indicate one or the other of these levels. Having the concept now, he gathers in to it examples which before would have escaped his notice. So there is continual interplay between Levels 1 and 2.

Parental Love and Discipline. This is where it all begins. The right side of the model pictures the motivational aspect of learning, and it begins at the first level with the parents' dealings with the child. In Psalms and Proverbs we read in several places about the fear of the Lord. It is the beginning of wisdom, the beginning of knowledge, and the fountain of life. How do children learn to fear the Lord? By first fearing their fathers. We saw in Chapter 3, through the teaching of Scripture and also from the psychiatrist Bettelheim, that early parental training is important to the conscience, and that conscience is necessary for learning. This means not only the learning of good behavior, but any kind of learning. The order, then, is first to fear parents; next, fear God. This enables the child to learn and arrive at wisdom and knowledge.

We see a close connection between learning and parental discipline in the Greek word *paiduo.* No English word is quite like this. Sometimes it is translated as learn, teach, or instruct, and other times translated as chasten. Can teaching be chastening or chastening be teaching? In this word it is. To see better what this might mean, let's switch the translations around in several familiar verses. Let's say teach where the English says chasten and vice versa. Remember, it's all the same word. Here are the results: "And Moses *was chastened* in all the wisdom of the Egyptians" (Acts 7:22), "and [Paul] *was chastened* according to the perfect manner of the law of the fathers" (Acts 22:3), "whom the Lord loveth he *teacheth* . . . for what son is he whom the father *teacheth* not?" (Hebrews 12:6,7). Our word *learn* formerly was used to mean both learn and teach. At one time a parent might have said in threatening tones, "I'll learn you." But this use is no longer current.

When parents have done their chastening-teaching job well, teachers find that children are already motivated to learn. They simply step into the parent's place and continue the teaching process. Teachers are part of the family system. Christian educator D. Campbell Wyckoff has said that our Sunday schools seem always to be like the family in spite of our efforts to make them like schools. Maybe we should stop trying to push them into the school mold and just let them be family. This fits better in our biblical theory of learning.

We can see the church as an extended family. Families pool their efforts and money to set up day schools, Sunday schools, clubs, camps, and other programs for the children's learning. They also should pool their disciplinary efforts. This means, first of all, that the teachers must care a great deal about the children. They will be like uncles and aunts and grandmothers to them. A commitment to teach, then, is not simply a commitment to the Lord and the Christian education board to perform certain duties. It is a commitment to the children as well.

A large church with a superbly functioning Sunday school has a full measure of this family quality. Junior teachers in this Sunday school give much time to the children they love. They not only teach each week, but they attend planning meetings and give two Saturdays per month to department activities of swimming, skating and so forth. Most teachers take the jobs as husband and wife teams, so the outings are family affairs for them, too. On Sunday morning the teachers are on their jobs early. The nurseries cooperate in this by opening one-half hour before Sunday school.

All this commitment of time and love pays off in good behavior and increased learning on Sunday morning. The child who picnicked with his teacher the day before is not likely to come in rebellious and boisterous. There are fifty or more children per classroom, but each child checks in with the secretary, goes to his own table, may walk about on social errands or turn in his homework and so forth. Such a dignified atmosphere prevails that a visitor from the more hectic kind of Sunday school might think he's in the wrong place.

All over the church are signs of this family feeling—an usher's hand on a young boy's shoulder, a teacher hugging a little girl, adults speaking to children in the halls and elsewhere. Now if you are a child surrounded by so many family members, you don't have much chance for acting up. If you and a friend sit together in church you might as well forget about whispering and rattling papers because whoever is nearby will hush you up. If he's not your teacher this year maybe he was last year, or at least he probably taught somewhere at some time and he's in the habit of checking behavior that begins to get out of line.

This is the church operating as a family.

This example is not meant as a formula for other churches to follow. Particularly, it is not meant as an argument that if teachers give lots of time a Sunday school will achieve a family feeling. The quality of time spent with the children is probably more important than quantity. Research has shown this to be true for working parents, anyway.

But this church has both quality and quantity of teacher time. And the church takes discipline seriously at all levels, right on up to the pastor. When a teacher wants help with a particular child, the department heads and others on the educational staff become involved. If they can't solve the problem together, the parents are contacted and asked if they have any ideas for handling it. If the problem persists and it appears that the parents need help in disciplining their child, that calls for pastoral visits and family counseling. Classes on rearing children are offered intermittently and the pastor preaches on the subject from time to time.

A church operating as a family can absorb a few "strays" without their parents, just as you can add a couple of children to your dinner table on occasion. But if the percentage of these grows too large, and particularly if the children are from undisciplined families, special measures are called for. Churches which bus in numerous such children often have elaborate systems for rewarding learning and good behavior. Much teaching time is used in scoring, passing out prizes or tokens, operating the token store, and so forth. All these techniques are borrowed from the behaviorists, and sometimes Christian educators argue on a philosophical level about whether or not this is "right." But seen from a psychological standpoint, some such system is necessary. It is simply that with undisciplined children the way to start is to teach them discipline. Instead of using behaviorist techniques for this, it would be an interesting experiment for some churches to work out a *Reality Therapy* system. This system is explained in a book by that name written by William Glasser (New York: Harper and Row, 1965). Children in reality therapy earn more responsibility and more privileges as they show they can handle them. This fits our Christian beliefs better than the behaviorist system does.

On our learning model, discipline is the base and all arrows point outward from this. The arrow pointing upward indicates that the discipline that parents and teachers provide leads gradually to self-discipline. The arrows pointing to learning Levels 1 and 2 indicate that children with discipline can learn on both these levels.

Heart-Set and Self-Discipline. On the basis of imposed discipline in the early years, the child develops his own inner discipline. Through most of the growing years this is an on-and-off discipline. That is, in some situations and in some matters a child can manage, but in others he still needs the help of parents and teachers to impose discipline from outside himself. The teacher needs to keep a balance. The child can be allowed freedom when he handles it well. But he should have structure and discipline when he needs it.

The arrows pointing outward to all levels of learning indicate that with the motivation of self-discipline children can learn at any level. They can learn as much as their abilities and opportunities will allow. The arrows pointing back inward indicate that learning experiences help to build further self-discipline.

Some learning rewards immediately. That is, it gives pleasure in some way and this is reinforcing, encouraging the child to learn again. But by this model, learning does not depend on reinforcement, as it does in behaviorist theory. The "reality principle" also operates. By the reality principle, disciplined children can work for rewards that are postponed. Children with more self-discipline need less outer rewarding and outer discipline.

Wise Self-Direction. Heart-set and learning merge into wisdom. The fear of the Lord was its beginning, instruction was its growth. "Give instruction to a wise man, and he will be yet wiser: teach a just man, and he will increase in learning" (Proverbs 9:9). The time can come when people take charge of their own learning and use their knowledge creatively. Junior children can experience this kind of learning from time to time. It doesn't happen by scheduling a twenty-minute creative expression period. It happens as an outgrowth of solid learning at Levels 1 and 2, in children who have a fair amount of self-discipline, in classrooms where there is an appropriate amount of freedom. Of course it happens outside the classroom too.

Creativity is a much overused word in our day. A teaching method or a teaching gadget is not creative just because someone labels it so. Only people are creative. You do your most creative teaching when you do what your heart says is right for your children. First, of course, you learn much at Levels 1 and 2. You know thoroughly the content you want to teach. You know your children well, too. And your lesson is prepared. Then comes a time in the classroom when things click just right. You seem to know what is in the children's minds and you are sure you're getting through to them. You almost feel something passing from your heart and mind to the children's hearts and minds. At such a time you are acting creatively. Your heart and your knowledge merge together in a creative teaching act. That is what is shown at the top level of the model.

Very young children can experience this top level of creativity, too. A preschool child, for instance, may be creative as he plays with blocks. He has previous knowledge and concepts of the blocks and of the garage or whatever he is building. And he can use that Level 1 and Level 2 learning in a creative way. So this top level is not a label for people. We don't say that finally John or Jane has reached the creative level. The label at the top is for a kind of learning, and it can happen at all ages.

This has been a brief description of the learning model to give an overview of its three levels and its two sides. The following chapters show various ways to use it.

READING CHECK

1. Moses gave explicit instructions about what teaching methods to use.   T F

2. Writers usually agree on which teaching methods Jesus preferred.   T F

3. This model of Christian learning theory describes both learning and motivations to learning.   T F

4. This model describes three levels of learning.

    T F

5. This model shows that junior children are usually on the middle of the three levels of learning.   T F

6. This model shows that being creative is better than learning "facts."   T F

7. This model shows that discipline and heart-set are important motivations to learning.   T F

8. Children gain inner discipline by first having outer discipline imposed on them.   T F

Answers: 1–F, 2–F, 3–T, 4–T, 5–F, 6–F, 7–T, 8–T

7 Using Questions

● *Questions are never easy to make, but it does help a little to know more about questioning and question types. In this chapter you will have some fun first reading about Socrates, who is supposed to have invented questions. Well, almost. Next, you will look into two junior classes where one discussion flops and another discussion goes pretty well. And last, you will learn three basic levels of questions, which correspond rather closely with the three levels of learning shown on the model in the previous chapter.*

Questioning is an age-old activity of teachers. Socrates is often mentioned as an ancient example, almost the originator of questioning as a method. But one might wonder if Socrates didn't have some rather clever fore-runners, because it is difficult to imagine one man inventing the method and also developing it to such an extent. And one also wonders if Plato wasn't at times writing with tongue in cheek.

Socratic questioning is really a form of argument wherein one leads his "opponent" by labyrinthian routes through a topic. In Plato's *Republic* Socrates asks his friends, "As concerning justice, what is it?" A long conversation ensues, and one portion reads as follows, with Socrates asking the questions and Polemarchus answering.

You think that justice may be of use in peace as well as in war?

Yes.

Like husbandry for the acquisition of corn?

Yes.

Or like shoemaking for the acquisition of shoes,—that is what you mean?

Yes.

And what similar use of power of acquisition has justice in time of peace?

In contracts, Socrates, justice is of use.

And by contracts you mean partnerships?

Exactly.

But is the just man or the skilful player a more useful and better partner at a game of draughts?

The skilful player.

And in the laying of bricks and stones is the just man a more useful or better partner than the builder?

Quite the reverse.

Then in what sort of partnership is the just man a better partner than the harp-player, as in playing the harp the harp-player is certainly a better partner than the just man?

In a money partnership.

Yes, Polemarchus, but surely not in the use of money; for you do not want a just man to be your counselor in the purchase or sale of a horse; a man who is knowing about horses would be better for that, would he not?

Certainly.

And when you want to buy a ship, the ship-wright or the pilot would be better?

True.

Then what is that joint use of silver or gold in which the just man is to be preferred?

When you want a deposit to be kept safely.

You mean when money is not wanted, but allowed to lie?

Precisely.

That is to say, justice is useful when money is useless?

That is the inference.

And when you want to keep a pruning-hook safe, then justice is useful to the individual and to the state; but when you want to use it, then the art of the vine-dresser?

Clearly.

And when you want to keep a shield or a lyre, and not to use them you would say that justice is useful; but when you want to use them, then the art of the soldier or of the musician?

Certainly.

And so of all the other things;—justice is useful when they are useless, and useless when they are useful?

That is the inference.

The twists and turns of reasoning have other humorous results. At one point the conversation comes to this.

And so, you and Homer and Simonides are agreed that justice is an art of theft; to be practised however 'for the good of friends and for the harm of enemies,'—that was what you were saying?

No, certainly not that, though I do not now know what I did say . . . "

The discussion seems to come to an end and Socrates reflects how he has gone from one subject to another.

And the result of the whole discussion has been

that I know nothing at all. For I know not what justice is, and therefore I am not likely to know whether it is or is not a virtue, nor can I say whether the just man is happy or unhappy.

But Socrates does want to persuade his friends "that to be just is always better than to be unjust" so the discussion resumes again. At one point they decide that it is easier for a state to be just than for an individual. They talk about the state, and Socrates comes to his famous statement that cities will be good when philosophers are kings or the kings and princes are as philosophers.

Near the end of the book Socrates gets his sparring partner, Glaucon, to agree that "justice in her own nature has been shown to be best for the soul in her own nature." Having agreed that justice is a good for its own sake and not for its rewards, they go on to affirm that there are rewards, too, both from men and the gods.

Thus writes Plato. The questions and answers are a form of thinking. They are a process of logic. They organize the argument. Though the Socratic method is sometimes mentioned and listed as a teaching method, it would be a rare classroom that used this method today. This may not even be appropriate for our classrooms, being a suitable pastime for old thinkers instead.

Another old method of questioning is the catechistic method, wherein the teacher asks series of questions and the pupils respond with memorized answers. This method is widely frowned upon today, being derogated as rote learning, meaningless learning or low-level fact learning. Some of this criticism may be unjust. As pointed out in Chapter 6, fact learning is necessary and important. Putting fact, or information, learning into the first level of learning is not to value it less than other levels, but is simply to categorize it as the type which usually comes first. It is the type upon which the next level is built.

Catechistic learning in itself is not the main problem. After our polls and surveys today we often lament that so many people do not know the basic facts of their religion. So it's not the teaching of basic facts we object to. And there is nothing wrong with question and answer memorizing. What really bothers us is for the catechistic method to become the whole of the teaching and learning. We want the students to do something with the facts, to personalize them, and to integrate them into their higher thinking.

Skillful questioning can help to accomplish this. Teachers can become more effective as they learn about various kinds of questions and their many uses. Later in this chapter we will look at three main types of questions you can use. But first we will look at some classroom examples of teacher questions in discussion settings.

The first example shows the futility of throwing out a high-level question for a group not practiced in thinking at this level. The teacher's first question is aimed at eliciting an application. The children have just read the story of Esther, and the teacher asks, "What is the meaning of this story for you?" To answer this, requires relating many things in the story to find something broad enough—a generalization—that can have application beyond the story.

As you read the transcript, picture a class with usually several hands raised. So when the teacher calls a name she is simply acknowledging one whose hand is raised. She is not arbitrarily calling on child after child as it may appear on paper. She only occasionally does this, trying at the first to get things going, or trying to draw out a child who is not volunteering. This teacher follows some other good discussion procedures. She is accepting of students' contributions and she does not dominate with her own ideas. She even waits at times five seconds so as to include the kind of thinkers who do not volunteer within the first two seconds. But this discussion never really gets off the ground. The children cannot handle the question before them.

TEACHER: What did the story mean to you, Debbie?

DEBBIE: Umm, I can't think.

TEACHER: Tom?

TOM: Well, it was exciting.

TEACHER: Exciting. What did it mean to some of the rest of you? Greta?

GRETA: The way Queen Esther helped her people.

TEACHER: Anything else? Mandy, what did you think the story meant? (No answer.) Eric?

ERIC: Well, just about Queen Esther. No, not just about Queen Esther but about Haman and Queen Esther.

BOB: And Mordecai.

TEACHER: Bob thinks Mordecai is important too. Debbie, do you remember now?

DEBBIE: Yes. That you shouldn't hate people.

TEACHER: Why do you say that, Debbie? Will you explain why you thought it meant that?

DEBBIE: Well, Haman, he hated the Jews.

TEACHER: All right. Cindy?

CINDY: Well, at the end, what the story meant to me was Haman, well he wanted to kill the Jews so he was killed himself.

TEACHER: Tom, you wanted to say something.

TOM: Well, see, like Mordecai, well he just helped the king to save his life, and Queen Esther wasn't afraid to go, and the king could order anything. That's all.

TEACHER: Greg?

GREG: When Queen Esther went to the king's big, uh, throne room he loved her and he held out his scepter.

JON: And she didn't have to die.

TEACHER: Jon, what did you say?

JON: She didn't have to die.

TEACHER: Yes. Lisa?

LISA: Well, in every Bible story there's a lesson, and in this story there's a lesson too. That you shouldn't do bad things.

TEACHER: So you think the story had a lesson to teach us. Any other thoughts about the meaning of the story? Debbie?

DEBBIE: You shouldn't want to do bad things to people.

TEACHER: Roger?

ROGER: You should love people.

TEACHER: Any other ideas? Ralph? (No answer.) Did
            you all like the story?

STUDENTS: Yes.

TEACHER: Why did you like it?

STUDENTS: Because it was good.

In another class, the teacher worked out a discussion plan that might be diagramed as in Figure 12. In her plan, focus 1 concerned Haman. All the facts the children could recall about Haman were to be marshalled together to help form their concept of the man Haman. Mordecai was focus 2. Then these two men were to be compared. Some thinking at this level would give the children a basis for drawing an application or meaning for themselves.

The plan worked out to this set of basic questions.

OPENING: What happened in this story?

FOCUS 1: What happened that told you what
          kind of man Haman was?

FOCUS 2: What happened that told you what
          kind of man Mordecai was?

RELATIONSHIPS: What differences do you see
          between Mordecai and Haman?

APPLICATION: Do you think this story has a
          meaning for us?

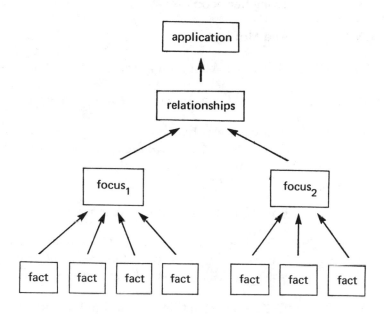

Figure 12

Other plans, of course, could be made. Focus could be made on Esther or on other persons or events. The culminating question could concern God's care for the Jews or some other big idea. But this plan was chosen, and these questions are the ones the teacher kept before her as she led the following discussion. This was in a sixth grade class, as was the preceding example. Again, picture a class, larger this time, with many hands waving. The teacher calls individual names to keep only one talking at a time.

TEACHER: What happened in this story? Fred? (opening)

FRED: Well, a lot of things. It's about Queen Esther saving her people.

IVAN: And Mordecai.

TEACHER: Mordecai? What about Mordecai?

IVAN: He helped too. Helped save the people.

TEACHER: And what else happened?
(The discussion continues a few moments on the first question. We take it up again further along.)

HUGH: Boy, Haman was really a mean man.

TEACHER: You think he was mean. Let's talk about
(focus 1) Haman for a while. What happened that told you what kind of man Haman was? Matt?

MATT: Well, you could tell what kind of guy he was. He wanted to kill all the Jews.

TEACHER: Any other ideas? Peggy?

PEGGY: He hated the Jews.

TEACHER: Anything else in the story that told you about Haman? Ivan?

IVAN: He wanted everyone to bow to him.

TEACHER: Hugh, what were you going to say?

HUGH: The same thing.

TEACHER: Okay. Who can think of something else?

Wendy?

WENDY: Well, I remember something. It might not be what you want. It's a little thing, maybe, not important, but he bragged to his family and said how great he was.

TEACHER: He bragged. That's important. Now let's
(focus 2) think about Mordecai. What happened that told you what kind of man he was? Fred?

FRED: Well, he worked in the king's palace.

TEACHER: Kristi?

KRISTI: He put on sackcloth and cried for all the Jews.

TEACHER: Ivan?

IVAN: Well, he cried and stuff, but he did a lot of other things for the Jews. He told Esther she should go to the king and if she didn't go she would get killed anyway so it's all right if the king might kill her.

TEACHER: Wendy?

WENDY: The king loved her so he wouldn't kill her.

TEACHER: Yes. Is there anything else that told you about Mordecai? Hugh?

HUGH: Well, he kinda, well, you know, he was like a leader and sent letters and things to all the Jews.

TEACHER: Kristi? I see you have something to say.

KRISTI: Yeah. Well, he took Esther, sort of like adopted her, and he didn't have to do that, and so, and he did it anyway, and it tells us what he was like.

TEACHER: Yes. Now what would you say are some
(relation- differences between Haman and Mordecai?
ship) Matt?

MATT: Well, for one thing Haman wasn't, he wasn't a Jew and Mordecai and Esther were Jews.

TEACHER: Haman wasn't a Jew and Mordecai was. Give us some other ideas. Peggy, you have one?

PEGGY: Well, that's why he hated them. And Mordecai didn't hate people. That was different.

TEACHER: One of them hated and one didn't. Wendy?

WENDY: Well, I think, well, Mordecai helped the king. Like it said in the books, he saved the king's life.

NATALIE: Well, I think you could say Haman helped the king too. He was, what you call it, like second ruler in the kingdom. That's helping.

TEACHER: So you think they both helped the king. Do you see any differences in the way they helped? Wendy?

WENDY: Yes. Maybe it's not, but I think Mordecai was, well, he was loyal to the king.

NATALIE: Maybe Haman was loyal too. How do you know he wasn't?

TEACHER: Aaron? You want to answer that?

AARON: I think the king would rather have Mordecai working for him. He could trust him. He wouldn't do anything bad.

TEACHER: You think the king could trust Mordecai more than Haman. What was different about Haman?

AARON: Well, I . . .

TEACHER: Kristi?

KRISTI: Haman was just interested in being great himself. He probably wouldn't think about the king so much.

TEACHER: (application) All right. So this story told you a lot of things about Haman and Mordecai. Do you think this story has a meaning for us? Hugh?

HUGH: Well, not to be like Haman.

TEACHER: Aaron?

AARON: It does a good job of showing about a good man and a bad man, and in the end it came out, well, both of them got what they deserved.

TEACHER: Matt?

MATT: Well, yes it has a meaning, and I think it

shows how people can be mean to you sometimes but God works it out in the ending.

TEACHER: Fred, you wanted to say something?

FRED: Well, I think it has a meaning because it was
kinda like a miracle. Esther was made queen
just in time, like Mordecai said, just so she
could save the people.

JOE: God made it happen.

TEACHER: You say God made it happen. What are you
really saying about the meaning of the story
for us?

JOE: I'm saying, uh, well, God could do it for us
too. I mean if we were in trouble and everything.

TEACHER: All right. Peggy?

PEGGY: Well, I think it does a good job of showing
how some people don't realize about quite a
few things.

TEACHER: Now can you be more specific? What don't
they realize about?

PEGGY: Oh, things like God and . . . They don't
realize that they shouldn't hate and . . .
I mean, I know you don't get saved by
being good, but, but . . .

TEACHER: But you think we should be good anyway?

PEGGY: Yes.

TEACHER: All right. Joe?

JOE: They don't realize that they can't just get great by themselves. I mean, God makes it. Haman was bragging that he did it.

In thinking about this last question the children generated a meaning beyond the actual story situation. They built their meaning on facts and relationships brought out earlier in the discussion. Every question sequence will not necessarily lead to an application question. Some other kinds of culminating questions are those which call for conclusions, summaries and inferences. The choice will depend upon the teacher's purpose.

The questions in the preceding example are planned according to the three thinking levels. The first three questions are intended to draw out information, the fourth is to help the children work at understanding the information better, by seeing relationships, and the last question is to help them use their learning—both the information and the relationships—in finding an application for the story. According to the thinking levels, then, we have this classification of questions.

1. Remembering information.
2. Understanding information.
3. Using information (and understandings).

A more detailed classification according to kinds of thinking is given in *Classroom Questions* by Norris M. Sanders (New York: Harper and Row, 1966). Sanders presents seven kinds which, except for some slight adjustments, are based on the six kinds of thinking that Bloom has identified in his *Taxonomy of Educational Objectives* (New York: David McKay, 1956). Both of these books are valuable study for anyone who makes tests, plans lessons or curriculum, or in other ways is deeply involved in these matters. But here we present a simpler way to look at questions, believing that a simpler system will be more usable for more teachers. Let's take a closer look at each of the three types.

1) Remembering Information. The mental activity required here is memory of facts. They can be "small" facts or "big ideas."

> What city did Joshua conquer first?
> Name the three parts of Joshua's military strategy.

They can ask for recognizing the correct answer, which is easier to do, or recalling and supplying the correct answer, which is more difficult.

> True or false. Saul was the first king of Israel.
> (Saul, David, Samuel) was the first king of Israel.
> Who was the first king of Israel?

They can ask for facts which were learned by Level 1 thinking or they can ask for facts or concepts which were learned by Level 2 thinking.

> Name the five books of Moses.
> Tell what kind of man Haman was.

There is a tendency to speak of "just facts" as though to devalue this kind of learning and to classify it as poor education. But no one has come up with a plan to eliminate facts. And if this is poor education, we all are guilty. Actually, we need fact level learning in order to go anywhere else with thinking.

This first level of questioning corresponds with Bloom's "knowledge" category and with Level 1 on our learning model.

2) Understanding Information. The mental activity required here is to think or act on information in ways that show an understanding of it. Translation is one common way of accomplishing this. A student may translate from words to words.

Tell in your own words what this verse means.

He may translate from words to diagram or map or vice versa.

(Looking at a chart of kings) Who was the first king of Israel?
Show on the map where Jesus walked that day.

Students may translate information into drawings or skits. Or they may begin with drawings and translate into verbal meaning.

Find the inner room which is called the most holy place.

Relating is a second way to show understanding. The students can relate facts by making generalizations, defining, comparing, showing cause and effect, and numerous other ways.

Which man does not belong in this list?
   a. Jeremiah
   b. Ezekiel
   c. Jehoshaphat
   d. Isaiah

How was Samuel different from Eli's sons?

Tell some ways in which the story of Noah and the flood is like the story of Lot in Sodom.

This second level of questioning corresponds with Bloom's "comprehension" category, and with Level 2 on our learning model.

3) *Using Information.* The mental activity required here includes logical and creative thinking. The student solves problems using specific information he has learned, or using original creative thinking. He applies his learning to new situations. He analyzes, synthesizes, and makes judgments, all on the basis of good information and learning, not simply as uninformed opinions. He is aware of the thinking processes required in these operations.

The fuzzy line between the more difficult Level 2 questions and the easier Level 3 questions is determined partly on this last feature. Does the student know what is involved in his thinking—in making good judgments, for instance? At Level 3 he does not simply give his opinion as his judgment, but he understands the need for criteria and for justifying his judgment by reference to the criteria. Another difference between Level 2 and Level 3 is that Level 3 thinking involves wholes. Whereas a Level 2 comparison question might call for comparison of Bible men to notice that some are prophets and some are kings, a Level 3 comparison question on Bible characters would include much more of the life or reign or message of each man.

Above the fuzzy line are questions that definitely call for creativity on the student's part. A common type is reading a true-to-child-life situation and asking what the child should do. Even better are the student's own real life situations. What meaning does a lesson's Scripture have for the student's actions or thinking or inner life? To do this well, that is to do it at Level 3, the students first need to be thoroughly conversant with the Scriptural principles. Much Level 1 and Level 2 learning has to take place first. Otherwise such a question is not really a Level

3 question. It only produces shallow thinking and pat answers.

This building up to Level 3 takes time. A sixth grade class was studying the Sermon on the Mount. One Sunday the topic was "turn the other cheek." The teacher tried the translation technique and application all in one assignment. She said, "Write in your own words what it means, and then tell an example." Here is one result.

It means if someone hits you on the right cheek, turn and let him hit you on the other cheek. For example, if your brother doesn't clean the room, well, maybe he will clean it next time.

That translation could hardly be called a translation, and the illustration missed the mark too. So the class stayed on the topic for a few more Sundays. The second Sunday the teacher tried giving her own translations. A boy remarked with feeling, "Nobody lives that way." It was a breakthrough to the second level. The boy related the Bible verses to real life. He showed in this remark that he not only knew what the verses said (Level 1), but he understood what they meant (Level 2). His comprehension was demonstrated by relating the verses to what he observed in life around him.

The teacher gathered examples of people who do live that way. She brought a clipping about a Christian school soccer team whose players turned the other cheek and played fairly and cheerfully while their opponents deliberately injured several players so as to remove them from the game. She brought stories of Christians in communist countries who suffered oppression, and torture, yet returned only love to the communists. Bible examples were used too—Stephen, Paul, Jesus. The class began to see that people can live that way and do live that way. They could see ways to apply the verses in their lives with siblings (roomates especially), school-mates, ball teams and other areas.

Of course this does not necessarily mean they applied it in their behavior (although some did). We are speaking here of cognitive levels of understanding. We are talking about intellectual application, not behavioral application, in this instance.

Another type of Level 3 question is synthesis. This is using facts (Level 1) and understandings (Level 2) in a creative way. A synthesis question in a junior workbook may say to the student, "Write a good title for this paragraph." There is no one correct answer in a question that calls for creativity.

Still another type of Level 3 question is evaluation. Here is an example of an evaluation question. Note that it must be preceded with study of creationism and evolutionism. Knowledge of these systems (on a junior level) is the criteria against which to evaluate the statements in the exercise below.

Decide if each item below would be said by:
_B_ one who believes the Bible.
_E_ one who believes in evolution.
_N_ neither.
____ 1. God made the world.
____ 2. God made Adam first and then made animals for him.
____ 3. The first men knew no language.
____ 4. Men nowadays are much better than early man.
____ 5. Blood must be shed for man's sin.

This third level of questions corresponds with Bloom's categories of application, analysis, synthesis, and evaluation. On our learning levels it is often Level 2 but its aim is to reach toward Level 3.

For those interested in the categories of Bloom's

TYPES OF QUESTIONS

Bloom's Categories of Educational Objectives	Sanders' Categories of Classroom Questions	Beechick's Simplified Question Categories
Knowledge	Memory	Knowing Information
Comprehension	Translation Interpretation	Understanding Information
Application Analysis Synthesis Evaluation	Application Analysis Synthesis Evaluation	Using Information

Figure 13

educational objectives or of Sanders' questions, the chart (Figure 13) shows the correspondences of these with the three-level questioning system presented here. We have seen in this chapter how teachers' questions call for different kinds of thinking from children—remembering information, understanding information, and using information. We caution, again, that having categories or levels does not imply a higher value for the higher level.

Research on questioning continually turns up the discouraging (for Americans) finding that children learn more when low level questions are used than when high level questions are used. One likely reason for this result is that teachers have learned to use higher level questions, but they have not yet learned that they should be used sparingly—only when the children are ready for them. Much spadework at Level 1 should precede Level 2, and much spadework at both these levels should precede the occasional Level 3 question that we use. This principle cannot be emphasized too strongly at the present time.

The first type of question we can hardly avoid. Many of our questions will call for remembering. We need to know if our children have the basic facts. This is a relatively easy part of teaching. It is harder work to frame Level 2 questions that will show us if children understand the information. The third type, questions that call for using the information in prescribed ways or in creative ways, are sometimes not difficult to think up, but we have a difficult job in preparing children to handle these questions.

Questioning has been important from at least Socrates' time down to our time. It is a wise teacher who works on developing this skill.

READING CHECK

1. The first level of questions is aimed simply at eliciting information.   T F

2. Some first level questions call for recognizing the correct answer, and some call for supplying the correct answer.   T F

3. Research shows that we use first level questions far too often.   T F

4. Second level questions help us see if children understand information.   T F

5. Second level questions call for translating or relating.   T F

6. Research shows that children learn more with high level questions than they do with low level questions.   T F

7. The key to successfully using third level questions is to spend much time first making sure the children know and understand the information.   T F

8. Level 3 questions should be used more often than they are.   T F

Answers: 1—T, 2—T, 3—F, 4—T, 5—T, 6—F, 7—T, 8—F

8 Using Organizers

• *Organizers are just what they sound like. They organize the learning. If these little organizers at the beginning of each chapter have helped you know what's ahead and helped you get a little more out of your reading, then you've got the idea already. In this chapter you will see first how important they are, and how they help move learning from Level 1 to Level 2. Then you will see some examples for juniors.*

A teenage Sunday school teacher one day was leafing through her new junior lesson book. There was Abraham. She remembered the story of his call and obedience. There was Isaac. Yes, the servant brought him the bride he met by a well. There were the twins Jacob and Esau, and the bowl of pottage that had some strange meaning about a birthright.

The teacher had learned Bible stories through her own years in Sunday school and Vacation Bible School. She knew most of them. But in leafing through the book a sudden insight flashed in her mind. "Oh!" she said to herself. "These men are all in order. They're lined up in the same family." If her teachers had ever told her that, it hadn't sunk in. Sunday school stories had always been a scattering. Adam here, Noah there, hairy Esau, brave David.

Of course the insight that the patriarchs were "lined up" was only a beginning. The teacher had to go on later to see still larger ideas, such as God's redemptive plan unfolding through His chosen people.

In our day the art of teaching individual Bible stories has developed to a high degree. As literature teachers begin with fables to teach children to get meaning beyond the literal story happenings, so we teach Bible stories. Every Bible story has a meaning. For us. This week. This analogy learning could be Level 2, but often it is Level 1, as children learn the pat answers that we should believe God like Abraham, obey God like Noah, and serve God like Samuel. As beginning literature students, children can find "meaning" in all their stories.

The meaning part is easy for us to teach. The "this week" part is harder but we manage. God may not call us to a new land this week but He calls us to Sunday school. There's a handy, weekly thing. God always wants us to do that. Or we might explain that heaven is our promised land. Does someone need to be saved today and answer God's call?

Some of this teaching strains the stories a bit, but much of it is worthwhile. Children need it when they are at this early stage of Bible learning. But we don't want them stuck in this stage forever. There are more mature things that juniors can learn—particularly, juniors who have already been well taught for several years in Sunday school or in Bible clubs and Christian schools. They need to go beyond the ideas gained from individual stories to the "big ideas" gained from larger viewpoints. The term "big ideas" here is not to value these as more important than "little ideas" from individual Bible stories. It is simply to categorize them as ideas which require a wider knowledge base.

Big ideas come in all sizes and colors. Some of them are theological, such as God's redemptive plan for the world. Some are historical, such as the special place of Israel in human history. Some cover short time periods and others stretch from eternity to eternity.

Here is one literature professor's view of the place of the Bible in teaching literature.

> . . . the Bible forms the lowest stratum in the teaching of literature. It should be taught so early and so thoroughly that it sinks straight to the bottom of the mind, where everything that comes along later can settle on it. That, I am aware, is a highly controversial statement, and can be misunderstood in all kinds of ways, so please remember that I'm speaking as a literary critic about the teaching of literature. There are all sorts of secondary reasons for teaching the Bible as literature: the fact that it's so endlessly quoted from and alluded to, the fact that the cadences and phrases of the King James translation are built into our minds and way of thought, the fact that it's full of the greatest and best known stories we have, and so on. There are also the moral and religious reasons for its importance, which are different reasons. But in the particular context in which I'm speaking now, it's the total shape and structure of the Bible which is most important: the fact that it's a continuous narrative beginning with the creation and ending with the Last Judgment, and surveying the whole history of mankind . . . in between (Northrup Frye, *The Educated Imagination.* Indiana University Press, 1974).

Taken out of context, the above sounds like a Christian statement. But in context, Frye does not appear to believe that the Bible gives The View of the world and human history, simply that it gives the best articulated view we have in ancient literature. Now if even that is considered essential for the education of a non-Christian, how much more it should be for the Christian.

We can teach the Bible to our juniors so thoroughly that it sinks straight to the bottom of their minds. But we can go farther than that. The Bible view can grow in their minds so it comes to unify all thinking. Education systems and philosophies all reach for an integrating factor, a central view to provide oneness and wholeness. Christians have that. A Christian education can be the strongest of all educations.

To achieve this we need to use intellect to its full potential. In our learning model, heart has an important place, but this does not mean that the psychological, "feeling," part of the child and his lessons is uppermost.

One of the functions of heart is motivation for learning knowledge and gaining wisdom (Ecclesiastes 1:13). With right heart-set, the intellect can soar higher and farther than it otherwise could. We must remember God gave intellect, too.

Some movements in Christian education tend to be anti-intellectual. They view with suspicion any learning that can't immediately lead to a "decision," or a "changed behavior"—this week. Or they include in the curriculum only those items that they believe will meet a psychological need (as we currently understand needs). But these approaches give only a partial education. We need the balance of intellectual approaches to Bible learning.

To teach the Bible intellectually one of the most effective things we can do is to organize content into "big ideas." The teenage teacher managed her own organizing of the patriarchal period because she was continuing to study and because she had an analytical mind which was inclined to organize things anyway. She had long had a nagging feeling in her mind that she really didn't have a good picture of the Bible. So her mind, perhaps largely subconsciously, worked on this problem and when the chance came to pull together some learnings into a unified system she had the "aha" experience that is such a pleasure to learners. This is Level 2 learning. It is relating facts that were learned at the first level. It is conceptual learning (Level 2). Some would call it discovery learning.

There is a lot of talk these days about discovery learning, but most that passes for discovery learning is counterfeit. The genuine thing is rarer than we suppose. To test whether the word is counterfeit, try using the word "find," or use "find out" if the context refers only to facts. If these words work, then real discovery learning is not in view, but you are only reading jargon.

J. R. Suchman is generally credited with first describing the pleasure of discovery and he developed a method of inquiry learning to attempt to achieve this experience more often. ("The Child and the Inquiry Process," presented at the Eighth ASCD Curriculum Institute, Anaheim, Cal., 1962.) Suchman's method was inductive, but others have achieved discovery results deductively.

Strictly speaking, discovery learning belongs to those who believe that knowledge is what a person structures within himself, namely, the humanists, while insight or concept learning belongs to us who believe that the Bible and God's handiwork constitute knowledge that we can gain. In the first, knowledge is only within a person. In the latter, knowledge or truth is "out there" anyway, whether a person knows it or not.

But whatever words are used, one important principle holds true in all the methods that have been proposed for achieving higher or deeper understandings. That principle is that there must be a basis of information. The learner must be familiar with the material before he can reach for the higher level of learning. To put it in terms of the learning model in Chapter 6, there must be a basis of Level 1 learning in order to build understandings at Level 2. This principle is another way you can determine whether some discovery learning you are reading about is genuine or counterfeit. Does it build insights from a basis of information? Or does it simply involve the children in finding information?

This basic learning should be carefully planned by curriculum workers and teachers so that it will lead to major concepts that we want to teach. We need to set up for conceptualization, and lead children to the concepts. We should use big ideas, frameworks, overviews. We need to use these organizers appropriately, not neglecting to put enough flesh on a framework to make it meaningful. All of us have read textbooks which were insufferably dull because they skimmed over the history of a people or nation not stopping anywhere long enough to put some real, live flesh on the framework. In Bible teaching our flaw may be just the opposite. We may be stopping everywhere and giving all kinds of flesh but never providing a view of the structure.

Insight or conceptual level thinking is exciting to juniors. Understanding relationships is not a strong point of primary thinking. But it emerges in the junior years. For an illustration of the excitement it can engender we will turn to an ordinarily dull topic—the multiplication tables.

A fourth grade teacher was letting her children experience multiplication by use of coin-shaped "counters." If a child needed to know 7 x 8 he made 7 piles of 8 and then he counted them. By this means the children worked out their daily problems. It was slow, but meaningful. A child knew what the 56 stood for when he wrote it down. And the 7 x 8 was not simply a string of symbols.

A boy named Galen thought of a shortcut. He wrote down 7 x 8 = 56. The next time he needed that answer he didn't have to count 7 piles. This pleased him, so he wrote down other combinations and was delighted to finish his daily problems more quickly.

One day he said, "I think I'll write all of them down and not use counters anymore."

"That's a good idea," said the teacher. "I'll show you a way to put all the answers in a box." She proceeded to draw the familiar multiplication table form and start him off. "Now when you make your piles of two, put the answers in this row. The piles of three go in this row, and so forth."

Galen was excited. The teacher's help was timed exactly right; he was ready for it. He set to work and filled in his whole box. Then he began showing it off to his classmates. "Look," he said, "I have all the answers in a box." And he explained to them how it worked.

In the next few days most all the children busied themselves making their own boxes. The teacher suggested they call them the multiplication tables. The classroom seemed charged with excitement over multiplication tables for some time. The final step was less exciting, but it made sense. If you memorized all the answers you didn't already know, then you could do your problems faster yet. You didn't even have to look on the table. And memorizing wasn't too hard. If you forgot 6 x 6 you could figure it out by working from 5 x 6. These children knew the relationships.

Galen and many of the others experienced second-level learning. They saw the relationships for themselves. They could not have done this without the knowledge base built from their experience with the counters. And they might not have done it as quickly, or perhaps not at all, if the teacher had not given them an "organizer" at the proper time.

This technique of using organizers is probably the most neglected feature of our junior level Bible teaching. We generally do a good job of providing a knowledge base of facts. But many of those facts will slip away without organizers to help hold them by giving them more meaning. Think what would have happened to the fourth graders' multiplication facts if they had never organized them into a meaningful whole. Many facts would not be recoverable from their memories as time went on. Each isolated fact would have to be worked out again laboriously. And some children would even have forgotten how to do that. (Of course repeated use helps hold facts, and multiplication facts are often retained this way, but time puts a limit on how much use we can make of the repetition technique for remembering.)

A junior Sunday school teacher had some boys in her class who loved math. She suggested to them a project (organizer) of making a graph of the life spans of men in the lineage from Adam to Noah. This had hardly begun as a class project before it developed that each boy wanted to do his own. So the project spilled over into the week.

The following Sunday the boys excitedly compared their graphs (Figure 14). Some unrolled long strips of graph paper. Others had smaller charts. "Look! Methuselah could have talked to Adam." The boys and their classmates saw that people not too long before the flood could have heard about God directly from Adam or from preacher Enoch. But they became wicked anyway. A number of relationships—meanings—became clear on the charts. Methuselah's death line and the flood line came at the same point. Of this "coincidence" the teacher explained what some commentators say on the subject: Enoch, in naming Methuselah, had prophesied that at his death the judgment would come. Methuselah's extra-long life, then, seems to show God's grace in delaying judgment so that men might repent.

Some readers at this point may be objecting that this early history is not to be taken quite so literally, that the data given are genealogies and not chronologies. If they are genealogies it would permit us to assume that some generations could be missing and the time span longer than it first appears. If they are chronologies, we could assume no missing time. We would see the data as intending to record time, as it seems to do in the technique of stating the father's age when his son was born.

But no matter which view you want to teach, the children need to begin with the base of information actually given in the Bible. These boys had the information and had it organized. In later studies of other genealogies and later debates on this issue they would always start from a higher position of knowledge and understanding than if they had not had this experience.

As the boys discussed their graphs, the question arose about how many people might have been flooded. These math buffs argued about how to figure it out. "The average family has about three children." "But in pioneer days there were lots more—maybe ten or twelve."

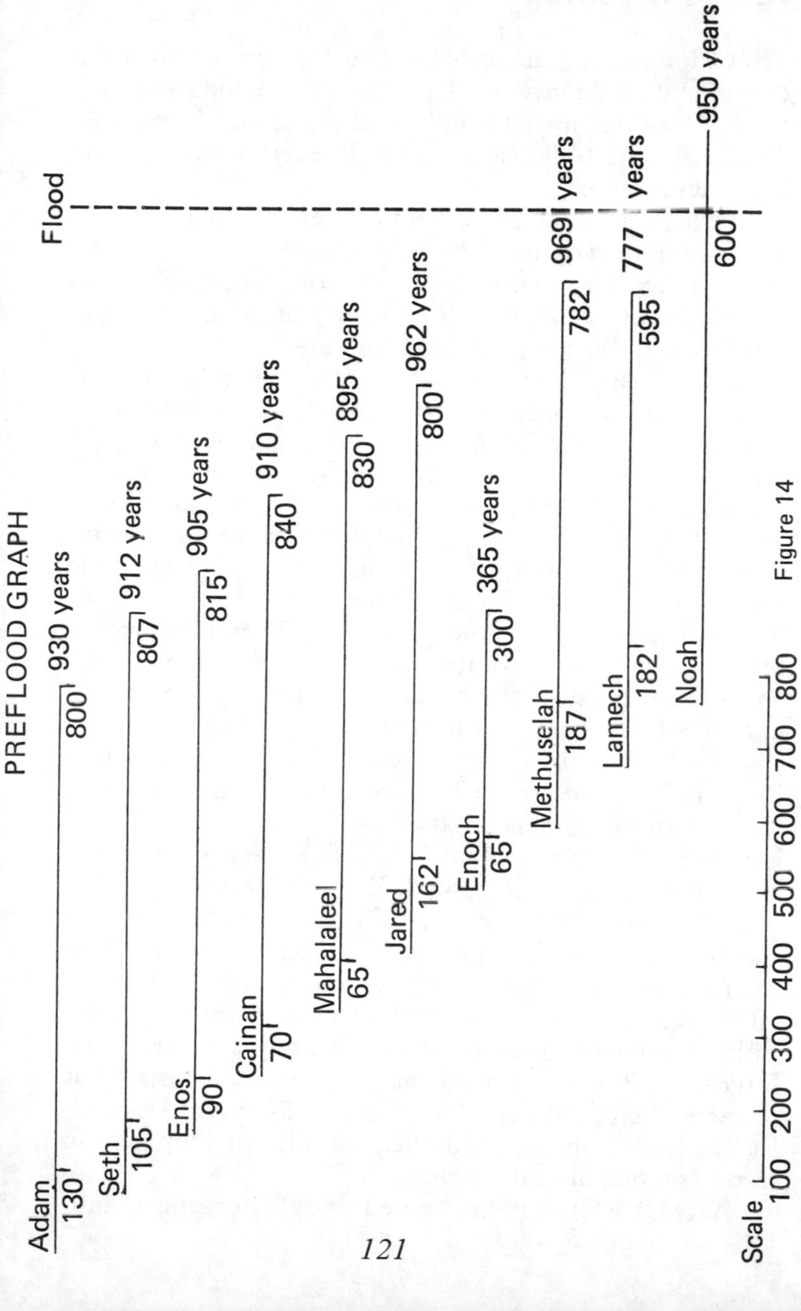
PREFLOOD GRAPH
Flood
Adam
130
800
930 years
Seth
105
807
912 years
Enos
90
815
905 years
Cainan
70
840
910 years
Mahalaleel
65
830
895 years
Jared
162
800
962 years
Enoch
65
300
365 years
Methuselah
187
782
969 years
Lamech
182
595
777 years
Noah
600
950 years
Scale
100
200
300
400
500
600
700
800

Figure 14

"How long is a generation?" The teacher supplied her opinions, too, to give what guidance she could. Each boy worked out his own formula, and pages and pages were filled with multiplication figures. Pocket calculators had not been invented yet.

This is an example of third-level learning—creative self-direction. The boys thought up their own problem and planned their own means of solution. Such third-level learning seems to fall as happy accidents in classrooms where the atmosphere is conducive to it.

Second-level learning is understanding relationships. And the use of organizers often makes this happen. It worked effectively in the case of the graph. A seventh grade teacher in that same Sunday school gave a test to his incoming classes to determine how much they knew about the Bible. One section of the test asked the students to mark whether an item belonged before the flood or after the flood. There were people—Adam, Abraham and others. And there were events to mark—building the tower of Babel, expulsion from the garden, and others. Most of the children from the "graph class" did remarkably better on the test than others.

Some children, without the graph, will relate certain items in their minds. They may think, "Adam and Eve were at the beginning of the world and the flood came later." So they could mark "expulsion from the garden" as occurring before the flood. But most juniors do very little relating and they can only do the test by pure guesswork. Their background of Bible stories may be considerable, but their ability to relate them in time is nil. And even their memory of them is likely to be low. Isolated events or persons or facts of any kind are easily forgotten. But a fact with many associations around it is remembered better. The more meaningful, second-level relationships not only help recall, but they help in reconstructing or in reasoning.

A child who sees his "graph people" organized into

a set of preflood generations, and who sees Abraham as the father of Israel (in another organization) has no trouble deciding that Abrahm must come after the flood. But a child who has not developed skill in relating or organizing operates simply on the fact level. Does he know the fact about where Abraham belongs? If not, there is nothing to do but guess or leave the answer unmarked.

Such historical chronology is a most obvious type of organization for Bible learning—particularly in Old Testament—and we need good organizers to help children develop these understandings. Teaching events in order is not sufficient in itself. The teacher noticing in her lesson book that Abraham, Isaac and Jacob came in historical order, no doubt had learned them in order in her own junior years. Nevertheless, they just fell into the jumble of Bible people in her mind. This is what will happen with practically all juniors. Very few will ever make larger conceptualizations without the guidance of the teacher. And the most effective means of providing this guidance is to use organizers.

Now, in using organizers we can't always use the involvement or inductive method as in the graph example. If we did, the children would get very little of the Bible organized in their junior years. Besides, the excitement would wear off. They would tire of the drudgery of figuring out charts and outlines and lists.

So we can supply organizers ourselves, and build our teaching around them. Figures 15, 16, and 17 show some of the variety these can take.

Some organizers are linear. Figure 15 shows an overall time line. As Professor Frye has said of the Bible, it begins with creation and ends with the last judgment and surveys the whole history of mankind in between. The time line is not detailed and complex, but provides a minimum number of "pegs." All juniors could memorize these pegs and learn to hang their future Bible learning in

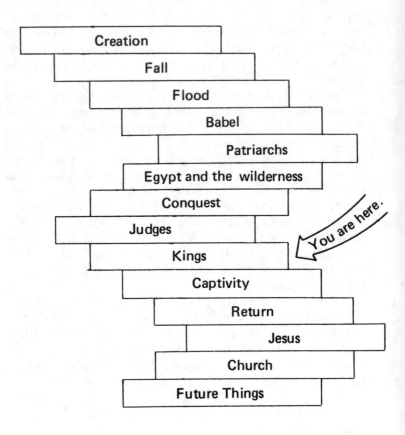

Figure 15

CHART OF THE KINGS

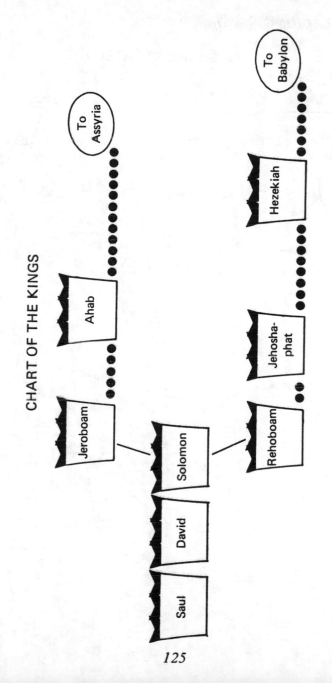

Figure 16

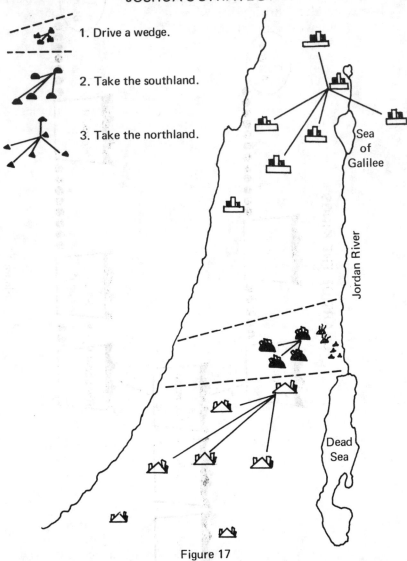

JOSHUA'S STRATEGY

1. Drive a wedge.

2. Take the southland.

3. Take the northland.

Sea of Galilee

Jordan River

Dead Sea

Figure 17

126

the proper places. The time line can serve to organize what children already know of the Bible, and it can serve as a framework or structure for future learning.

This latter quality of organizers—that of structuring learning—shows another reason why children cannot always "discover" and make their own organizers. Bible scholars, curriculum designers and teachers need to go ahead of the children, providing framework, showing them structure, and speeding them on their way as they build their own learning.

Some organizers depart from a straight line into more complex charts. Figure 16 shows a Y arrangement. The united and divided kingdoms of Israel are pictured through their successions of kings. This illustrates well the curriculum principle of learning the overall structure, and learning only selected portions of it in depth. Here you see certain crowns enlarged with names on them, and other crowns merely pictured. Children in this unit of work will learn about the times of the kings by concentrating on these selected kings. If every king and every event are given their full weight here, the study becomes cluttered with a mass of details so that the structure itself falls from the weight of it. But when the structure is well built during junior years, the child can in later years come back and fill in with more learning at any point he wants to.

Again, it is not enough just to arrange the lessons in order and emphasize the kings which are shown. The children, as well as the teacher, have to see where the lessons are leading. They have to know the structure. Repeatedly during their study of kings they should see the chart. They should work with it in various ways. At some time or other during these activities many of the children will experience conceptualization. All the children, whether they see it at Level 2 or merely learn it at Level 1, should in the end have it quite well memorized and be able either to draw a chart or fill in names on a blank chart that is already drawn.

Some organizers are maplike. This goes far beyond the ordinary "Let's find Jericho on the map." As with the line and chart organizers already described, a map organizer must be worked with repeatedly and thoroughly. This is even more important with map organizers, since maps are complex productions to start with and junior children are only beginners in understanding maps. Map organizers can be used to show the wilderness journey, the captivities of Israel and Judah, the Gentile kingdoms, the spread of the early church, and other Bible matters.

With maps we should not assume that lights flash on in our children's heads when we locate a city or trace a route. It doesn't work that way. Through our long experience with maps and traveling and meeting people from other places we have built a pretty good equation between a map of the world and the real world. So we might have that light-flashing experience. A missionary points out where he worked and we say, "So that's where Borneo is," or "That's where Fairbanks is." We have the large structure already waiting, and it only remains for the new fact to fall into place.

But with juniors we must remember that we are building their structure. To do this we need to be much more creative in our use of maps than most of us have been in the past. Figure 17 shows a map organizer of Joshua's conquest. Through their lessons the children learn the three-part military strategy: 1) drive a wedge through the middle, 2) take the southland, 3) take the northland. The lessons flesh out the main parts of this framework. But, as explained with the kings chart, they do not get lost in too many details. At the same time the children are learning the fleshy parts—the stories of the conquest—they also are working repeatedly with the framework. They label, color, draw, enlarge for bulletin board, and so forth. They memorize the three-part strategy.

A considerable body of research shows that more learning happens when there is good use of organizers. This is an area we need to give more attention to, not only at junior ages but at all ages.

READING CHECK

1. Christian education can be stronger than secular education because everything can be integrated into a central, unified view.　　　　　　　　T F

2. Junior children are too young to think of total world history from creation to the final judgment.
　　　　　　　　T F

3. As a rule, junior children do very little relating of facts without help from the teacher.　　　　T F

4. It is best to give organizers first, before the facts.
　　　　　　　　T F

5. It is best to give organizers last, after the facts.
　　　　　　　　T F

6. Organizers might come at any time in the learning; a good teacher senses when the time is right.　　T F

7. The best way to have discovery learning is to let the children learn and discover on their own.　　T F

8. On a framework some parts should be learned in detail to provide flesh, and other parts should be passed over.　　　　　　　　T F

9. Junior children understand maps well since they have had them in school.　　　　　　T F

9 Using Published Curriculum

• *The first part of this chapter will help you know how to choose teaching materials. You will find some basic but often misunderstood information about published Sunday school lessons. And you will find out what the major considerations should be as you choose among them. Then the latter part of the chapter gives suggestions for getting good use from the materials you select.*

For early Jewish education the rabbis wrote the Talmud. The word *Talmud* means *instruction* or *learning*.

When the Christian Sunday school movement began, the first curriculum materials were those used for teaching basic reading and writing to poor children who had to work the other days of the week. As social conditions changed, Sunday schools in England and America turned to teaching the Bible to all classes and ages of people. This new teaching required a curriculum, so a sequence of Scripture texts was chosen, and commentaries on these Scriptures were prepared for teachers' use. Here was a Christian "Talmud"—a unified curriculum for Sunday schools. Still later, Sunday schools faced the problem of slanting the teaching more specifically to various age groups, and graded curriculum was born. Henrietta Mears was a leader and indefatigable worker in this movement.

Now we have available a wide selection of curriculum

materials from denominational and independent publishing houses. Many are excellent, professionally prepared, attractive and colorful materials. The very multiplicity of these may be bringing us to a state of satiation. We find ourselves trying to choose among finer and finer points of differences in the materials. Some have opted out of the curriculum choice altogether and said, "We will use no curriculum; we will just use the Bible." But interestingly enough, a leader in such a Sunday school tells the teachers what to teach from the Bible, and a new curriculum appears in his head or on mimeographed sheets. Some of these eventually are published and add to the numerous choices already available.

So anyone using curriculum or selecting curriculum today must learn a few basics about curriculum language and curriculum issues so as to find his way around in this otherwise bewildering field. First of all, textbooks have come to make fine distinctions among terms like curriculum, curriculum plan, and curriculum materials. And there is the "hidden" curriculum in addition to the more open kind. But teachers and advertisers don't always stick with the textbook usages, so the distinctions are blurred in our common language. This is not a great loss except for people interested in theoretical matters.

In the last century, Rousseau popularized the romantic view of the child's flowering and growth from inside, teaching of content was downplayed (in theory at least, though not always in practice), and curriculum came to mean the total environment in which the child grew. But such a broad view of curriculum is impracticable to talk about when you're concerned with what to do in your own Sunday school and in your junior class. Most of us, when we talk about a math curriculum or spelling curriculum or Bible curriculum, mean the actual content with the materials and lessons which contain the content. In this chapter we will use the word in this narrower, more ordinary sense, although sometimes we will mention curriculum plans or materials, too.

Now that we have the language settled, we will turn to a few curriculum issues. A quick overview of certain of these issues will also help clarify the curriculum field and the choices we need to make.

One issue, which might have been dead, except that publishers have kept it alive, is the old issue of unified curriculum versus graded curriculum. Unified curriculum began, as mentioned previously, with the earliest Bible curriculums for Sunday school, when the one Scripture portion was taught to all ages. And graded curriculum came as teachers of children found the older plan inadequate for their needs. Publishers who produced graded curriculum developed their own plans, choosing content for each age group, the criteria for choosing varying among publishers. Publishers who remained with the unified plan also had to make changes. They kept up with the times by making lessons which were better geared to the various age levels. And they added lessons for very young children, who were not taught when the original unified lessons were in use. Since there was difficulty in translating lesson content chosen for older students into something meaningful for young children, the unified idea was used loosely and there ended up being quite a lot of difference in content at the different ages, anyway.

The result is that we now have curriculums called "unified" and others called "graded" which are not so different after all. And publishers, in order to sell them to us, have to play up what differences there are. One side says that everyone is learning what's appropriate for his age, while the other says the unified topic is geared appropriately for each age. One says that the whole family is studying the same topic, while the other says it's not appropriate for everyone to be learning that two plus two equals four. In one, Dad can see his children studying the same theme he is, and in the other, Dad can see his children learning what he learned when he was a kid. In one, family togetherness around the Sunday dinner table consists of a third hour of the same topic everyone talked about in Sunday school and heard the pastor preach in church. In the other, dinner table togetherness can begin with the question, "What was your lesson about today?"

Since everyone is interested these days in strengthening the family, both kinds of curriculum have included many features to help with this goal, and the curriculums become more alike than ever, while trying to sound different. The real difference between unified and graded curriculum is almost obscured in past history and it has only to do with the way content was originally chosen and organized into lessons.

Another issue in curriculum is that of age grading (or close grading) versus departmental grading. This, too, would not be much of an issue except that publishers (or books like this one) keep it alive. There really is not as much difference to you, the junior teacher, or to your Sunday school, as it may at first appear. But you do need to understand grading in order to use the materials in a way that best fits your school.

Even unified materials are graded, as explained above, so this matter of grading concerns all materials. Now the language you run into and have to understand includes the terms *age graded, closely graded, departmentally graded, junior department* and *middler department.* The first two terms really mean the same thing. Closely graded materials have a separate set of basic lessons for each grade, and it works just as in the public school or any graded weekday school. The children move on each year to the next set of lessons and the teacher stays in her grade and teaches the same lessons to the next class. Some teachers write to their publisher and say, "You sent me the same lessons I had last year. Don't you have anything different?" These teachers haven't realized that while the lessons are the same, the children are different.

This year's fifth grade class needs the fifth grade lessons the same as last year's class. If the teacher is tired of teaching them, she should ask for a transfer to another grade. Public school teachers often do this in order to vary their teaching life. But all teachers should understand that in graded curriculum the lessons are arranged by grades with the children in mind rather than with the teacher in mind.

Departmentally graded lessons are different from the public school plan. This plan was developed specifically for Sunday schools. Since many schools are not large enough to have a class for each grade, they combine fourth, fifth, and sixth grades into a junior department. More recently there has been a further subdivision of third and fourth grades into a middler department with only fifth and sixth grades in the junior department. Both kinds of school organization are in existence now. Schools tend to divide as much as they can according to their size.

To accommodate these departmental groupings, publishers have issued lesson material with labels to match. Thus you can buy material labeled for middler or junior department, rather than labeled for fourth grade. Now, does this all mean that large schools should buy closely graded material and small schools should buy departmentally graded material? No, not at all. Once you learn your way past the labels, you see that there is little actual difference between these materials.

When you have a class of fourth, fifth, and sixth graders, you can order junior lessons for them. The second year you can't use the same lessons because some of your children haven't graduated to the next department, so your publisher sends a second set of lessons, and the third year they send a third set. That is the full cycle. The following year they will begin repeating the cycle.

The departmental publishers cannot gear the lessons specifically to sixth graders or to any one grade, but they must build in enough choices and flexibility so you can manage with your mixed grades. Also a graded school could manage with these lessons, the fifth grade teacher teaching on a slightly lower level than the sixth grade teacher, but both using the same lessons.

Now if your department is ordering from a publisher which has closely graded lessons, almost the only difference is that you must do the cycling instead of letting the publisher do it for you. This procedure worries some teachers and they write to their publishers asking, "How can I have sixth graders in a fourth grade course?" The answer is that the publishers foresaw the teachers' problem. They know that many Sunday schools are not fully graded, so they, too, have built sufficient flexibility into the lessons.

So whether yours is a large church or a small church, you can use either departmentally graded or closely graded materials. There is not as much difference as the labels may imply. Closely graded materials do offer a bit more help in gearing the teaching for specific grades, and in sequencing content they may offer an advantage to those schools which are organized by grades. Departmentally graded materials, having the feature that all classes are on the same topic, allow a school to have "opening exercises" on that topic. Some see this as an advantage.

So far we have seen that there really are only small differences between unified and graded curriculum, and between closely graded and departmentally graded curriculums. A few other features can be dismissed, also, as of relatively minor importance for selecting curriculum. One feature often included on checklists is that of the fit at each age level. In former days that might have been a major difference between publishers, but no longer. Practically all established publishers have age level specialists who know how to plan good lessons for the various ages.

The same situation prevails in the area of teaching methods. Publishers keep up to date on these matters and, while the advertising may try to persuade you toward a curriculum on the basis of its use of one or another popular fad, you will find good lessons and good teaching ideas from most publishers today. Also, we need to understand the fact that the differences among methods are not as much as we tend to think. At least when we are speaking in large, general terms—i.e., activity method, visual method, mastery learning, lecture—a superiority of one method over another is not shown by research.

Another minor item which used to be included in checklists for evaluation of curriculum, is color and attractiveness of materials. The race for attractiveness has already been run and practically everyone has crossed the finish line. There is little need to judge in these matters anymore.

We have looked at some of the features which formerly were important in choosing curriculum, but which have lost significance in our time. So how do you choose a curriculum for your Sunday school? What is important to look for?

The major item to look for is the view of the Bible which the publishers hold. You will need as close a theological match with your church as you can find. If there are some minor differences of interpretation you can always adjust for these, but if you find yourself making too many adjustments it might be wise to look for other material. But move slowly and thoughtfully. Sometimes a church leader becomes upset over a sentence or two in a lesson manual. He writes the publisher an angry letter about the "error," and he vows to change curriculums. After the change he will soon run into an "error" in the new curriculum. Or, worse yet, he may realize after a year or two that there are a lot of topics important to him that never come up in the curriculum because of the publisher's effort to avoid controversial topics.

Denominational publishing houses provide a good theological match for many churches, but in some cases the materials from these are not up to the quality that can be obtained elsewhere. To get better quality, some groups have combined their resources. For instance, several denominations of Wesleyan theology have produced a joint curriculum. Publishing houses independent of denominational control may also adhere to a particular view, such as a Baptist theology. Independent publishers which are interdenominational manage their stance by treading carefully around certain issues.

These theological differences among curriculums should be one of your major concerns in selecting curriculum. A second major concern is educational philosophy. This is a relatively new concern, at least for groups which call themselves evangelical or fundamental. It is only in the last couple of decades that secular humanist approaches have begun creeping into Christian education materials. Humanism is a broad topic that cannot be handled at length in this book but is examined more fully in another book of this series, called *A Christian Psychology of Learning.*

The route by which humanism gets into good Christian materials appears to be this. Out in the secular educational world practically all basic research is carried on by humanists. Prominent developmentalists, for instance, believe that man is a product of chance evolution, that he is strictly biological and material, and that he has no soul, spirit, heart, or anything immaterial, as in our Christian beliefs. They have no belief in the supernatural. Based on these humanistic theories, many new approaches and techniques are developed for teaching. These have the aura of being "scientific," and this carries much weight even with Christians.

So the next step is that well-meaning Christians

incorporate these humanist ideas into their curriculum, probably without a good understanding that some of them tend toward enthroning man and dethroning God. This whole process is subtle and it's probably not possible to make a checklist that directs you to look for this, this, and this, and if you find them to throw the curriculum out as too humanistic.

One way to guard against this influence is to study educational theory and philosophy and learn more about these matters so we can more easily recognize these tendencies in curriculum. But this is not practical for many volunteer teachers, who have their own fields of work to study and keep on top of. If you are one of these, a more practical way is to keep up your personal Bible study and live as close to the Lord as you can. Then when your heart tells you that a teaching suggestion or an aim or something else in a lesson is not God-honoring, but gives an improper emphasis to self then you can take action. You can change the lesson so you are comfortable with it. You can teach what you know to be biblical and worthwhile. You can also make your objections known to the publishers. They do listen to teachers. And you have the additional option of selecting another curriculum which you find to be more solidly biblical.

In today's Christian education world, these two matters—of theological slant and of educational philosophy—are the most important ones to consider in selecting curriculum.

Now we will turn to the topic of getting good use out of your curriculum once you have selected it. First of all, remember that you're the teacher. You're the real, live person in the classroom with the live students. One teacher complained that he was having trouble teaching the full lesson in his manual. There was just too much each week and he couldn't complete it. A wise counselor said, "Remember, you are teaching children, not lessons." That remark radically changed the teacher's perspective of his task, and what had seemed a major problem shrank down to some simple decisions that he easily moved through. You are not a servant to the curriculum; it is servant to you.

And a great servant it is. If you have a home and family to care for and perhaps a full-time job, too, in addition to the volunteer job you have taken at your Sunday school, then published curriculum is one of your best helpers. Older books on teaching usually told how to plan a lesson from scratch. They told you to take a Scripture portion, to study it first, and then to go to commentaries and other books, to formulate your aims, and plan a lesson and gather materials. If you followed these and all the other instructions you would spend most of your week planning your one lesson. Even professional teachers don't do that. They have curriculum helps and thus manage to teach many lessons every week.

Besides the unrealistic time involved in this system, there are other weaknesses. For one, it sees teaching only in weekly, lesson-size segments. It never looks at curriculum from the perspective of a unit or of any larger scope or sequence for children. These older books sometimes failed to explain where the Scripture portion came from in the first place. If we assume it was chosen by a curriculum planner and given to the teachers, then the curriculum plan splintered off at that point into as many directions as there were teachers, as each teacher developed his own aim.

How different it is for today's volunteer teacher. Professionals have worked a full week and more to give the teacher a good lesson that fits into a well-planned curriculum for the child. Each teacher can stand on the shoulders of these full-time Christian educators and reach out from there, personalizing the lesson to his taste and fitting it to his own pupils in whatever way his good judgment tells him to.

Curriculum materials are the greatest and most

effective means for teacher education in the Sunday school world today. This is a little recognized fact. We tend to think that people are not learning how to teach unless they take courses or seminars or come to the staff training meetings. But new volunteers are always starting out, boldly or timidly or somewhere in between, and week after week they read the lesson instructions written by professional, experienced teachers. They see well organized lesson plans. They read the wide variety of teaching ideas for their age group. They try these with varying degrees of success. They study again each week, learning from past successes and from failures, too, and one day they wake up to the fact that they are not novices anymore, but experienced teachers.

That illustrates the first principle for getting good mileage out of your curriculum—the principle of really using it. If you are new at teaching, use it rigorously and learn all you can. If you are experienced, use it for the continuity it will give to your children's learning and for the time it saves you. Then use your saved time for building relationships with your pupils or in other ways going beyond what you find in the lesson books.

To prepare for using your lessons, you should read the introduction and other teaching helps. Introductions are not for skipping. Usually they are packed with information you need. Find out if your lessons are organized into units. If so, familiarize yourself with the total unit before you prepare the first lesson. Is the course a survey? A detailed study of one Bible character or one portion of Scripture? Is it topical? Or does it move chronologically? You need the total picture and you need to get the general aims in mind before you dive into preparations for lesson 1. It is good even to know what the overall curriculum plan is for other grades besides yours. Where do your studies fit into the total?

You can pass some of this information along to your pupils, too. They like to know that their lessons are going somewhere. This need for structure and an organized feeling was seen in Chapter 8.

When you have the big picture, the overview of your new course, it's time to begin preparing lesson 1. Sit down with pencil in hand and your Bible alongside your manual. Read the lesson from both your Bible and your manual. You will find that the manual adds pertinent information from research sources and it mentions other parts of Scripture which add meaning to the lesson. These are some of the time-saving features. This way every teacher doesn't need his own large library of Bible commentaries, dictionaries, and books on history, archaeology, ancient languages, geography and other related topics, and he doesn't need to spend large amounts of time researching. You will find, also, that the Bible lesson in the manual at times omits some details of the Scriptural account. This is necessary to keep most lessons to a manageable size and to keep them aimed toward the major teaching goals. It is not in any way devaluing Scripture; it is only that in selecting Scripture to teach not everything can be selected at once. As you read the Scripture portion you can tuck these extra details into the back of your mind somewhere. Occasionally a question will come up in class that you can answer with this information. Also, it gives you a feeling of being really on top of the lesson. You always should know more about a topic than you plan to teach on it.

As you read in your manual, underline, make notes in the margins, cross out parts you plan to skip, list materials you may need to gather. Personalize the lesson for you and your particular children. Do you have a testimony that will add meaning to the lesson? Make a note to tell that. Does the lesson call for some equipment you do not have? Plan a substitute method. For instance, if there is no chalkboard or overhead projector, get large sheets of newsprint and write with charcoal or felt pen. Better yet, see if your church might add chalkboards to the classrooms. Is there a game or other active learning method that takes more space than you have? Figure out a way to adapt it to your limited space. For instance, many circle games can be adapted to ordinary classroom seating by having children come to the front of the room instead of the center of the circle. If your class consists of three children and the lesson calls for a team relay, you can let two children race to complete the task while the third child acts as judge. Then repeat the race again with a different judge. Though you find many good ideas in the manuals, you do need to use a bit of ingenuity yourself.

When the manuals suggest methods that are new to you, see these times as opportunities to expand your teaching skills. Juniors are generally willing to try almost anything, so if an idea sounds good to you, you can confidently urge them to try it. Together you may feel you are embarking on an experiment. Teaching experiments sometimes work out great on the first try. Other times they may need additional tries, perhaps with a little adjustment in the procedures. But in any case, they add zest to classroom life, and help you view teaching from a slightly new perspective each time.

In addition to reading your manual you should read the student lesson book. Most of these books have work which is to be done right in class, and all instructions should be clear for you. A variety of procedures can be used. When a story needs to be read, you can have children read silently, then follow with questions and discussion together. This way every child gets to read. But if you have some poor readers, the silent reading method should not be used. Have one or more children read aloud so that the poor readers at least get to hear the story. Then work on questions or other exercises in the books. Give plenty of help in spelling and other details, so that your slower children can do the work.

Children enjoy working with partners or small groups

sometimes. You can try this on certain workbook exercises. The group goal is to have everyone's answers correct. As children discuss the work and even perhaps argue about it, all will be learning. This is a good way to work a test sometimes. If attendance has been irregular, or if for some other reason you feel it will be too threatening or discouraging for children to work the test separately, use the team method. All scores are totaled to make the team score, so each student has an interest not only in his own paper, but also in his teammates' papers.

Some lesson books include homework. Or your teacher manual may suggest homework. The best single thing you can do to stimulate interest in homework is to make use on Sunday of what the students did during the week. Put yourself in their place. If you studied your lesson and brought it to class and no one ever looked at it or gave you opportunity to express the opinions or questions you formed during your study, how many weeks would you keep it up? Probably not very many. But if you found everyone using his homework in class you might manage to get yours done too.

Many teachers, putting themselves in the place of their students, have decided not to require homework routinely. Certain types of assignments seem more natural for homework. Sometimes a homework suggestion is for the child to tell someone what he learned in class—a prophecy about Jesus coming again, for instance. Sometimes it is to prepare something which will enrich the following week's study—a report, a puppet play, a chart or drawing.

Appropriate homework, in other words, is not just for the sake of having homework, but it is a natural outgrowth of class work or it contributes to the class in ways that the children can see. It also can usually be done better at home or at school than in Sunday school class. An example is an assignment to see what the school history books have to say about an ancient kingdom or something else in the Bible lessons. Let the children choose what homework they will do, and when they will do it. Such an approach to homework is more meaningful and gets better results than giving routine, weekly tasks, the same to all children regardless of their interests and abilities.

Many teachers use their memory verses in this routine way. Some manage to motivate students well enough that they get good results, and like the system, and do not want to change it. But others are looking for a more effective memory system. There is a better system available, and some curriculums now are beginning to build it into the lessons.

This method is called the "whole memory system." It has been developed around principles arising out of the research on memorizing. A description and summary of memory research is given in a full chapter of the primary book in this series, and it will not be repeated here, except to say that the research shows these three advantages for the system: 1) greater efficiency, 2) more meaning, and 3) longer retention.

To use the whole method, you first select a passage of Scripture. For your juniors you may wish to start with a small portion, but this system works with passages as long as a full chapter. The idea is to learn the passage as one piece, rather than learning it verse by verse by verse. The method has these four steps.

1. Become familiar with the whole unit.
2. Review the whole unit many times with concentration and with different approaches or contexts.
3. Put extra work on difficult parts, if necessary.
4. Overlearn.

If you want to try it, don't be discouraged at the slow start; remember it really is more efficient and will take less time in the long run than the part method will. You also will experience the other advantages mentioned earlier. You will find the passage becoming more meaningful, as you will see its organization and interrelations of the parts better. You also will be pleased to eventually recite smoothly through the passage. You will not stop after a verse and try to decide which verse comes next any more than you stop after g when reciting the alphabet to decide which letter comes next. It is all of one piece in your mind just as the alphabet is. Don't stop when you have barely learned the passage. Continue until you have overlearned it. For a time, review your passage every day. Then gradually space your reviews farther apart until once a year or so is enough to keep it. A high school student learned eight New Testament books during his junior and senior years, motivated by quiz competition. During college, one of his summer projects each year was to review all the books he knew. He also was adding more than the original eight, and the once a year review was adequate after he had overlearned and at first had reviewed more often.

Step 2 of the method is wide open to all the procedures a creative teacher can invent. This step is going over the whole passage with concentration. The high school memorizer decided simply to read a chapter five times each morning and evening. By the second morning he began trying to think ahead of his eyes as they glided down the page. Some might want to use a sheet of paper to gradually uncover the lines of type, "reading" from memory when they can and uncovering the lines when they need to. The memorizer who invented this system found that by the second evening he only had to look at the words a few times on each of his five readings. He practically knew the chapter already.

The real secret is in the concentration. You have to find a means to keep your mind from wandering. A junior teacher accomplished this by reading onto tape and using the tape while driving alone. She tried saying a phrase or more of the passage and when she got stuck she turned on the tape. It checked her recitation and then prompted her on the next part. At this point she turned off the tape and continued reciting until she got stuck again. This was her Step 2, after the familiarizing of Step 1.

In working with children we need to devise ways to get them to read and recite through their whole passage many times with concentration. The class can read together from a chart or from their Bibles. Fun gimmicks, such as reading softly, then reading loudly, work. The teacher can start each phrase or verse and let the children finish it. Children can recite to partners, the partner prompting as needed. All the learning games that you know or that may be in your lessons are helpful here.

While Steps 1 and 2 are proceeding, have lessons about the meaning of various parts of the passage. Not everything at once, but bit by bit add to the children's learning. When the passage is almost memorized give attention to the remaining difficult parts and help the children master these. Then don't stop as soon as a passage is memorized. Overlearn. And review in a gradually tapering off schedule.

The memorizer mentioned above who learned a chapter in two days began the reviews by reviewing daily for two weeks. Then he reviewed weekly for a time. Then he tapered off still more until his yearly summer review was enough.

Younger junior children should be led by the hand through all of this learning. They should be familiar with the procedure and the success it brings by having used it in their primary lessons, but most children this age are not independent workers enough to carry through such a long project. Older junior children, who can think about thinking, should be taught the method itself. They should understand its four steps. They can share with each other their own little inventions for doing some of the steps at home. But they still need teacher help. The class can be working on a passage together. They can do some work in class and at times have homework, too, to speed up the procedure.

Another kind of homework that children like is found in the supplementary materials that most publishers provide—take-home papers or paperback Bible story books. Sunday school papers have a long tradition behind them and paperbacks are a newer feature. Both have their advantages. Some teachers feel it is important to send a paper into the home each week. It is a follow-up for the lesson; it can be given even to visitors; and it is a silent witness in non-Christian homes. Teachers who prefer the paperbacks see them as more in step with the times. They are not throwaways, but with their more permanent look will stay around the home longer and be read by more people. They, also, follow up the lessons. If not each week, at least intermittently they provide review and enrichment beyond the lessons.

Most American churches in prosperous times felt that whatever money they spent on curriculum materials was worth it. They bought everything their teachers or pupils might have wanted, and they didn't always pay sufficient attention to whether the materials were being used well.

For less prosperous times, or for making money stretch farther anytime, here are some alternatives. With supplementary materials, such as paperback books, consider not just handing them out automatically to every child. After a quarter or two, when the books are not novel anymore there will be some children not particularly interested in reading them. Although the large majority of juniors love to read, there are always a few who don't. And there are a few who cannot read well enough to enjoy these books. Try making the books available and see who takes them. Or have the children pay a small amount to take a book. If they pay they may value it more and be more determined to read it. Or try having several copies available for checkout.

If the materials you buy are dated and will not be used again, find a way to recycle them yourself. Use posters and other desirable items for prizes. Take some materials to sick or absent class members. Make puzzles from the pictures. Find a mission organization which can use your teaching aids or leftover student books.

If your materials are undated and will be used again next year or after a two- or three-year cycle, be sure to save all your teaching materials as well as any unused student books you may have. So much money can be saved this way, that your church definitely should provide space for filing these. If everything is thrown away after the quarter, or allowed to get scattered and lost, this probably is the greatest single waste in your whole Sunday school budget.

Remember, it is illegal to save money by buying just one student workbook and xeroxing copies of it. Stealing copyrighted material helps nobody. Publishers are in the Christian education ministry just as you are, and they struggle to keep the cost to you as low as they can. One way to do this is to achieve volume sales. The more student books they print, the lower the cost of each book. So if a church cheats on paying their share of the cost they, in effect, are passing on their share to other churches who continue to observe copyright law.

There really is nothing unfair about copyright law. Nations have lived with it for centuries without feeling compelled to object or resist or change the system. There are international agreements on copyright law, and it is even mentioned in the United States constitution. Recently the laws have been revised to cover new technology, such as office copy machines. Organizations on both sides of the copyrights—both owners and users—were deeply involved in working out the agreements, and all are satisfied with the results.

But scattered here and there are a few Sunday school teachers who are not as informed on these matters as they need to be. One wrote to her publisher, "I wish you didn't feel as you do about your material and would let me copy it." Another wrote simply that she was copying the material in order to save money, apparently not aware of the unlawfulness of the act she was confessing. Some teachers seem to feel that they should be immune to laws and ordinary business affairs. "This is the Lord's work," they say as they decline to pay their bills for Sunday school materials.

What a poor, pinched-up attitude that is for a child of the King. And how much more honoring to the Heavenly Father it is if we all are completely ethical and law-abiding and businesslike as we go about His work. Let's save money in all the legitimate ways we can. Let's be good stewards of what God gives us, and trust Him to supply our needs.

Beyond the basic Sunday school lessons are a few more materials you should have. First in importance are books for the children. You should have books with a definite Christian message, and other books of wholesome reading. With a good selection you can keep the children reading your Sunday school books throughout their junior years, and you will squeeze out much of the dubious reading they might pick up elsewhere. Keep abreast of the children's need to make book reports at school, and have books appropriate for those whenever possible.

This is urgent; get started right away. Don't wait until you collect all the usual library supplies and find someone to process the books and so forth. One teacher began with an armload of books she carried about in a cardboard carton. The checkout materials were only a sheet of paper and a pencil. Children wrote their names and the titles they took. When they returned a book, they crossed it off. Be the kind of librarian that encourages children to read, not the kind that guards the books and is happy when they are neatly on the shelf, numbered, accounted for, and not lost. A good class outing is a trip to your local bookstore where every child gets to select one or two books. This starts your library instantly with books that are sure to be read.

Somewhere in your program there is a time of singing. It may be in Sunday school opening exercises or in children's church, or perhaps even in class. If you are helping to plan that, you will need to give some thought to what can be called the "music curriculum." Do you always sing children's choruses which were first learned in primary department and everyone knows, so the children request them or the song leader thinks of them easily on Sunday morning, but the repertoire is gradually diminishing so there are only a few which get used Sunday after Sunday? Or do you sing teen choruses because a teen leads the songs or the children like to sing what they hear from their older brothers and sisters?

Many Sunday schools fall into one or the other of these patterns, but with just a little thought and planning they could do better. Juniors are ready for a wide variety of music. Their diet should include classic old hymns and worship songs which are meaningful to junior age level, as well as the lighter choruses, Bible teaching songs and fun songs. Look for good new songs and good old songs and every once in a while teach your group something different. Expand their musical horizons, and don't just coast along on what other people have taught them.

Last of all, we will look at your private "bag of tricks." What do you do on those occasions when your planned activities are not working? Or when things just finish up too soon and there is nothing more to say? Or when everyone seems unusually restless? You can get them all jumping up and down, singing "Hallelu, Hallelu." Or you can get them all competing with a "sword drill." If you have more than these two tricks in your bag, you probably are above average for junior teachers today.

As you teach, you can gradually collect several more profitable, spur-of-the-moment things to do. Some ideas in your lesson books are the right kind to add to your collection. You can copy them onto file cards which you keep in your classroom, or into a notebook you carry with you. To add to your collection, you will find more of this kind of activity in a book written to fill this need, *While Waiting for the Bell to Ring* (Beechick, Accent Publications).

No other generation of teachers has had the plentiful curriculum materials that ours has. We must choose and use them wisely. But they, of course, cannot accomplish the teaching task without that most important person, the teacher. To that person we turn in the next chapter.

READING CHECK

1. The original unified curriculum was a plan wherein all students studied the same Scripture content.   T F

2. Later unified curriculum is a plan wherein all ages study the same topic or theme.   T F

3. Graded curriculum is a plan wherein content is chosen specifically for the various ages.   T F

4. Closely graded lessons provide separate lessons for the fourth, the fifth and the sixth grades.   T F

5. Departmentally graded lessons provide the same lessons for all grades in a department.   T F

6. There is considerable difference in difficulty level between closely graded and departmentally graded materials.   T F

7. Up-to-date teaching methods are about the most important thing to look for when choosing curriculum.
                                                            T F

8. Good color and art are also very important today in choosing among curriculums.   T F

9. Humanism is found in secular education but not

in Christian education.   T F

10. The whole memory system is more efficient than the part memory system.   T F

10 Styles in Teaching and Disciplining

● *In this chapter you will first look into the classrooms of Miss A and Mrs. Z. They are almost opposite in their teaching styles, and observing them will help you make decisions about your own teaching. Mrs. G will help too. Second, are some practical suggestions for classroom discipline, and last, is a description from research, of the best teachers.*

Miss A stood in front of her fifth grade girls with her Bible in her hand and the lesson manual in her Bible. She began to talk to the girls about David. With no special storytelling skill, but with simple conversational manner, she told the girls about David as a shepherd and a harpist, and about his anointing as king. The only break at all was two or three times when she asked one of the girls to read a verse. After they did so, Miss A explained the verses. She didn't ask the girls any questions. She didn't show pictures of the sling or harp or horn of oil. She didn't write the word *anoint* on the board so the girls could have a look at it. She didn't suggest an exciting project the girls could look forward to after listening, and she didn't try to stimulate interest in a homework assignment. When she was through talking, that was it. The lesson was over for the week and everyone was simply to walk out and come back again the next Sunday.

But one thing went wrong with Miss A's plan. Near

the end of the lesson she said something to the children about applying the Scripture to their lives. Elsa stood up with her Bible in her hand. At this display of decorum, Miss A could do nothing but recognize Elsa and let her speak. "I was reading my Bible," Elsa began, "and I found this verse." She read a verse about praise from Psalms. "And I applied it in my life."

"Good," said Miss A. "That's what we all should do." And she went on with her sermon about applying the Scriptures. She did not ask Elsa to tell more about how she applied the verse. She did not ask the other girls if they had similar experiences to share. She closed the lesson and the girls walked out for another week.

In the modern view of most of us that lesson had one bright spot which showed what a lively time of thinking and interaction it could have been if Miss A had a different idea of what a teacher should do. If you ask some of the elderly people in your church what Sunday school was like when they were children, you might get descriptions that are very close to Miss A's class. Some people remember such classes as insufferably dull. Others remember that they heard words which changed their lives—sometimes not while they were in the pew, but years later when the truths would not let them escape.

In another kind of Sunday school, Mrs. Z had learning materials placed around the room—all the materials prescribed in the lesson and more, because she believed in being creative. The children came in and they were creative too—not by belief, but by nature. Russell and Toby discovered the microscope immediately. But they weren't interested in the nature slides placed on the table with it. They began by putting drops of their own blood on the slides. They later got the idea of looking at girls' hairs. There was some squealing and hassling over this, but the teacher told the children to sit down and get busy. She was helping some children at a table with Bible learning games. The girls who lost some of their hairs to the boys were busy and quiet for some time doing something with the papers that were for drawing things that God created. They giggled a little, but not enough to disturb the teacher. In a few moments it became clear what the girls had done with the papers. They descended on the boys and began catching "cooties" from their heads. Two other teachers had arrived, so that disturbance was soon quelled. All three teachers worked for a time trying to get the children interested in the intended topic at each of the centers.

Later at group time, after songs and other preliminaries, the teacher tried to get the children to tell what they had learned about God's creation. There was little response. "Didn't you see all the little ribs on the onion skin?" asked the teacher. "What does that tell you about God's creation?" The children couldn't figure out, so she explained that God designed everything intricately and perfectly. The children did remember from kindergarten lessons or someplace that there were six days of creation. But they could not name what was made on each day, so Mrs. Z told them. Still trying to involve the children, she asked about other things God made for them. Thus, in group time they touched on the scientific idea of design, the historical idea of the order of creation, and the psychological idea of "What's in it for me?" It came out a sort of jumble around the creation topic. The children went into groups again, a teacher with each group, and they did a planned handwork project on the creation days.

The two teachers observed here differed in their idea of what teaching is all about. The first one felt that she only had to present a lesson to the children. And that was all she did. The second teacher felt that she should have activities for the children. And that was almost all she did.

Somewhere between these two extremes is where the best teaching lies. Many good lessons are close to the first teacher's style, but with some pupil participation added. Just a little recitation or discussion would have helped this lesson immensely. Recitation is telling information back to the teacher, and discussion is thinking and talking about the information in ways that go beyond it. Recitation uses mostly Level 1 questions and discussion adds Level 2 and Level 3 questions (see Chapter 7).

Either kind of participation would have helped the lesson in at least three ways. First, it would have provided feedback for the teacher. She could have seen, through children's answers, whether they had listened and understood and remembered. With feedback she could have seen whether they missed something or misunderstood something, and she could have retaught as needed. Without feedback she had no good evaluation of how the lesson got through to her pupils. She could evaluate herself: she wasn't nervous, she knew the material well, she had enough prepared to last the full period, and so forth. But she could not evaluate the pupils' learning. Even a brief written quiz at the end would have helped. For maximum learning from a quiz the pupils need to know the results quickly, not next week.

A second way that participation would have helped the lesson is in heightened concentration of the pupils. When children know they must answer questions later on, they listen with more purpose and more concentration. We would too.

A third way such participation would have helped is in providing reinforcement. Reinforcement is extremely important, and it possibly is the most neglected part of learning. A supervisor of teachers has said that the greatest difference between new teachers and experienced teachers is in their use of reinforcement. A new teacher tends to think that once the material is taught, it's taught. This happens with both the "lecture" type teacher and the "activity" type teacher. In the lecture classroom the teacher could have provided reinforcement intermittently during the lecture or at the end of the lecture, or both. If the children had answered questions, talked, and thought about the material their learning would have been much reinforced. Activities could have reinforced, too, some better than others.

In the super-large classes that some Sunday schools are having these days, careful thought should be given to the principle of reinforcement. The teacher can supplement his information and give variety by films, slides, transparencies and other projections. Main points can be summarized on a projected visual and the teacher can repeat them. The children may repeat with the teacher by speech or sometimes by motions. Sometimes it works to have the children form pairs and recite something to each other. A signal must be arranged for giving attention to the teacher again. Worksheets provide a good means for reinforcement in these large groups, and in small groups too. The children can all have pencils and worksheets and at various times throughout the presentation do their reinforcing work on them.

We have considered a few ways the lecture teacher could have improved her lesson. Now we will consider the activity teacher. First, of course, Mrs. Z needed better supervision of all the activities. But more basic than that, she needed a better feeling for the place of activities in learning. She had what might be called an over-belief in activities, thinking that as long as the children were active they were learning. Her goal was to have all kinds of activities for the students. Some of her activities related well enough to the lesson and others only in a fringe way. Some did not relate at all, but were available because she had gone to the work of making them, and she wanted to get use out of them, and they were, after all, called Bible learning activities.

Now, there really is nothing wrong with having a little learning on another topic besides the main topic of the day. An activity time could include other topics and in this way individualize the learning and tailor it to pupil needs. For example, a child who does not know the books of the Bible as well as his classmates do could be learning them during an activity time. An activity time could be used to stimulate interest in a new topic, perhaps to raise questions about something the class will be studying soon. So there is no need to have a rule that all activities must relate to the lesson of the day

The real problem in Mrs. Z's class was her attitude toward activities. They took up a major part of her class time simply because she thought that's the way a class should be. If she had a little of Miss A's belief in content and good organization of it she would have better lessons. If she understood that she needed to provide some Level 1 information before the children could do the Level 2 thinking and Level 3 work that she wanted, she would have stronger lessons. She would put more emphasis first on the Level 1 learning and on direct reinforcement of it. She probably still would see activities as ways to make the class enjoyable for the children, but she would see that solid, organized learning also gives the children satisfaction and pleasure.

Somewhere in between Miss A and Mrs. Z is a rather wide range of excellent teaching styles. You can develop your own style from what you truly believe about teaching and from what you know about dealing with your particular group of children. And you need not have one set pattern for your lessons. A group of your children may have high interest in the play they made about Samson last week. If that play needs performing this week let it be performed. You can't pour cold water on children's enthusiasm just to stick to your lesson pattern. If you encourage children's creativity by appreciating it you will find that more activities are initiated by the children. This is Level 3 learning. When you have that from time to time you find teaching as exciting as the children find their learning is. It's better than when you plan all the activities.

Mrs. G is one of those many teachers somewhere between the extremes of A and Z. She was teaching her sixth graders a unit on Joshua. She studied her lesson manual and her Bible, and learned more than her pupils, she said. We observe her on the week after the Jericho lesson. The class was looking at a projected map and she said, "Now, Joshua's strategy is to drive a wedge right across the middle of the land, so what do you think he will do next?"

"Take Ai," several answered, as it was quite clear on the map that this city came next in his path.

Mrs. G passed out worksheets which showed the terrain around Ai. "On these papers you get to pretend you are the general and you are planning strategy. How will you take Ai?"

The children bent their heads over the papers and busily drew soldiers surrounding the city, climbing the walls, attacking from the front, and other ideas. Some drew troops on horses, which they later learned Joshua did not have.

"Are you about ready?" Mrs. G asked a couple of times.

"Not yet," they answered.

Mrs. G worried that she was allowing too much time for this preliminary activity, but interest was so high that she really couldn't cut it short.

In time the children finished one by one, and each child who wanted to got to show his drawing and explain his strategy. Then they read from their lesson books what Joshua really did. And you can guess what good attention they gave to this story, and what good mental images helped them understand.

There was little time left in that lesson for the reinforcing activities Mrs. G had planned to use. She and the children talked a little about some of the most important points. Then the period was up and everyone, teacher and pupils alike, felt it had been a very short lesson.

In later lessons of the unit, Mrs. G didn't use introductory attention getters. Her children were so interested in Joshua and his exciting exploits that these weren't needed anymore. Some children were reading ahead in their Bibles at home just to see what Joshua was going to do next. In class Mrs. G had the children read the story for the week. Then she used the discussion and other reinforcement ideas in her manual, and had good lessons all through the Joshua unit.

A wide variety of teaching styles can work. Each teacher needs to be genuinely herself or himself. That self, and the style, may slowly change as the teacher gains experience, tries new ideas, reads books, and learns from fellow teachers. Every new idea is not better. Some ideas are tried awhile and rejected; some may not work this year, but if tried with next year's class will work fine.

Teachers, and pupils too, need time to adjust to new procedures. In Mrs. Z's class there were problems on both sides. The pupils were given more freedom than they could handle well, and the teacher planned more activities than she could integrate into the lesson. Both teacher and pupils needed the reins pulled in a little. In Miss A's class the reins could have been loosened. The children were well disciplined and could easily have handled a chance to talk, do research, play a learning game, or other classroom activity.

Some A-type teachers have difficulty adding activities to their teaching style. They simply don't believe that classrooms should have that kind of hubbub going on in them, and they feel guilty allowing it. Other A teachers, when they first try activities, are delighted with the results.

On the opposite end of the scale, we have today some Z-type teachers who know no other way to teach. They have heard the "gospel of activities" preached in training classes or seminars until their whole goal is to involve the children. The involvement goal may overshadow the learning goal. Such a teacher reasons that children busy in activities and interaction with each other are learning more. A professor showed the fallacy of this when he said, "I can pass out a worksheet with poor instructions on it and really score points for student interaction as they try to figure out what to do. But if I give clear instructions the students will work quietly and learn more."

It is helpful to know that teaching and learning are not at all the sciences they sometimes are presented to be. You need not be intimidated into thinking that it ought to be precise and smooth and scientific, and somehow you haven't arrived there yet. What counts, first of all, is that you apply your heart to the teaching God has given you to do. Now if your heart is in it, it follows almost automatically that you will want to really accomplish something with the children and not just fill in the class time.

It's basic, then, to know what you want the children to learn and to have a plan you believe will help them learn it. The plan your heart is in is the best one for you at this time. Later on, with more study and experience, and with some experimenting, your teaching style may gradually change. Published materials these days give you plenty of new teaching ideas to try, and their curriculum plans give you a systematic set of goals you may adopt or adapt for your particular class.

In discipline, too, you must put thought and work into finding methods that are effective. A class in Christian education practiced what they called discipline by taking turns teaching a Bible lesson while the rest of the class acted up as ornery children. They learned to intersperse the Bible lesson with commands, coaxing, threats, remarks in the category of "I love you and Jesus loves you too." They tried not to be sarcastic. They tried ignoring misbehavior and commenting on good behavior, which may work on children but doesn't work so well in a college class that understands the technique and that is having fun with the day's particular victim. These students, when they had classes of their own, would know how to apply Band-Aids when children left the path and fell into the briar patch.

A better approach is to devise systems that will keep the children on the path, and if they veer toward the edge, or even over the edge, the system should have ways to push them back onto the path. The first requisite is good planning for the class session. If the total time is prepared and run in businesslike fashion, a large percentage of the discipline problems will never arise. For some classes—particularly for the small, short classes that many Sunday schools have—this may be the only precaution needed.

If the class runs fine except for one or two students, these problems should be handled individually according to the type of problem. Look at what's happening and think through the best way to solve it. If a boy is not really defiant, but just cheerfully active and disruptive, it could be that he has difficulty sitting and listening as passively as the class may require him to. Try planning something more active, and give him the most active role of all. He may turn out to be a leader, pulling the other children along with his enthusiasm. If a girl is socially inept and antagonizes everyone with her name-calling and insulting remarks, try enlisting the whole class to help. Arrange an opportunity to talk with the class when she is not there, and say something like, "I want to talk to you about Jeannie. You know that she doesn't act good. Now, the rest of you all know pretty well how to act. You can be polite and kind when you want to, but Jeannie has never learned that. I'd like to ask you all to help me, because I can't teach her this by myself. What do you think will happen if all of us are as kind as we can be to her? When she acts mean, let's not be mean in return, but let's just keep showing her a kinder way to act." Allow a little discussion time about this, not to talk about how mean Jeannie is, but to talk about how it might be hard sometimes and how it may not work real fast, but may take a while. And the class members can agree to do this job together. Juniors love such a conspiracy. Many kinds of problems have been solved in this way and the conspirators usually learn more than the troubled child.

Some problems are too persistent and too disruptive to be handled in class. Though some teachers feel they should take abuse and show "love," putting up with a disruptive child and praying that he will be saved and change his ways, most teachers feel that a wiser love is more firm than that. One man pointed to a child and said, "You get out of my class and don't come back until you decide to act right." The boy walked out but returned the following Sunday and acted right.

Expulsion from class ordinarily should not be an impulsive act. The teacher, along with superintendent or principal or whoever may be involved, should carefully plan the options. Where is the child to go? If he is a pupil who walked in off the street, as in the above example, he can walk back out to the street. But if his parents brought him to Sunday school, or if it is a day school class, the situation is entirely different.

In a children's church situation, one church gives a warning for a first offense and on a second offense has an usher take the child to his parents in the adult church. The parents are then supposed to discipline the child at home in whatever way they see fit. The whole church understands this arrangement and is asked to cooperate in it.

Other possibilities are for the child to go to the equivalent of a principal's office or to an isolation room where he can complete a study assignment under supervision of a department superintendent or extra teacher. Since most churches have neither extra space nor extra teachers, an alternative is for two teachers to make a reciprocal arrangement. The sixth grade teacher may put her disruptive child in the back of a second grade room where he is to finish his worksheet and not participate in any class activities. The second grade teacher may on occasion bring one of her children to the sixth grade class. If he doesn't read well, he may not be able to do much work independently, but he can sit there a little frightened and feeling the disapproval of his older sister and her friends. They are not to include him in their class activities.

Sometimes the expulsion idea doesn't need any stigma attached to it. All that may be needed by some children is a little personal attention. A junior superintendent dismissed all the children to their classes and said, "Jerry, will you stay here with me?" She sat down with Jerry and said, "Your teacher tells me that you are so smart you answer all the questions and the other children never have a chance to answer at all." This was gilding it a little, but she continued, "So today we're going to have a class with just you, and you can talk all you want to." She led the discussion into the topic of salvation and Jerry was saved that morning. The next Sunday the two sat down for their private class again. In the middle of it Jerry asked, "Can I go back to the other class?" "Well," the superintendent answered, "we could try it if you can remember not to talk so much. Even when you know the answer, could you wait sometimes and let somebody else talk?" Jerry thought he could. The superintendent helped him make plans for how he would act in class, then she agreed to let him try it the next week. "I'll ask you afterward how it went. I think I'll ask your teacher, too, how she thinks you did."

That was the last private class Jerry needed. He

didn't change dramatically; he was still a very talkative boy, but with some reminding from his teacher he did make an effort to keep the talking under control. And the teachers had the joy of seeing the fine young lad continue in the Sunday school all through his teen years, even though he was a walk-in child, the only one from his family to come to church.

When the discipline problem involves only one or two children, put your head to work devising the best approach. Work with the child around the school and perhaps outside the school environment too. If you can't solve the problem consult with other staff members and with the parents. Several level-headed adults should be able to control one junior child in practically all cases. Some few may need professional counseling, medical treatment, special schooling, or other outside help.

Now if your discipline problem involves a whole class, you can't expel them all. You can get angry, and shout and threaten. Or you can try to carry on under duress, being meek and "loving." Or you can assert yourself as "boss" in the classroom. The first two styles are not recommended by most authorities, but the assertiveness style is recommended, and is once again gaining popularity among teachers.

To assert yourself, you set up basic rules and the penalties for breaking them, and you plan a system of rewards, too. This all comes from the behaviorist theory of learning, but it works in these situations. First, you explain that you are going to teach and no one will be allowed to stop you from teaching. Also no one will be allowed to stop others from learning. Then you explain the rules needed for this. Rules can be changed later, if necessary, and sometimes the children can help you make them. The rules should be posted in the classroom.

Penalties and rewards are explained, too. Day schools often use free time as a reward. Sunday schools have to come up with other ideas. Some use treats at the end of class. Good behavior notes to go home work in some neighborhoods. A flexible and widely used award is the token. Tokens are used later in a "store" to buy a choice of items.

Sometimes group incentives will work, and they are much simpler to manage. A point is chalked up on the board for good class behavior for five minutes. Or a marble is dropped into a jar. When a certain number of points are earned the whole class gets a treat.

These elaborate systems for obtaining good behavior may be necessary in some situations, but they are meant for children low in discipline and heart-set according to the learning model of Chapter 6. The long-range goal should be to move children to higher levels.

In situations where there are many poorly disciplined children a good plan would be to set up additional classes where the more disciplined children are allowed to go. In these, more time can be spent learning the Bible and less time learning discipline. These classes should naturally be more enjoyable than the others, and children who are ready for them will have the higher, inner rewards of learning and of being trusted and chosen for the classes.

Some discipline systems involve what might be called group counseling or group therapy. Teachers who are not psychologists should be cautious about experimenting with psychological therapy techniques. But there are group teaching techniques which fall more definitely into the teacher's domain. Simple discussion about behavior problems is often helpful.

Use Bible principles where they fit. Teach about using time for the Lord, about consideration for others in the class who want to learn, about respect for God's Word and for the teacher God sent to teach it. Just hearing these principles from you may not bring in the children instant, dramatic results. But this will have its effect, and these teachings are, after all, some of the reasons the children should act right. In discussions, some children will show that they really want well behaved classes. They will indicate that they don't like disruptive incidents. As you and these children show your thinking and attitudes the more disruptive children will be affected, and their attitudes will tend to change in the direction you want.

Roleplay is a technique solidly in the teacher's domain, although psychological counselors use it too. You can devise situations such as children bothering a child who really wants to study, or children heckling a teacher who is trying to teach. If your worst misbehavers volunteer for the teacher part or the studious child part, choose them. Let the children play a situation for a couple of minutes. Then call a halt and ask them to describe how it felt to be in their various roles. This is simply helping the child to step into someone else's shoes, and it can be quite eye-opening.

As a teacher you have many tools at your disposal for teaching content and for teaching behaviors. You never need to throw up your hands and say, "Well, what do you expect from this neighborhood?" or "With his kind of problem, you can't really expect any better." Go ahead and expect better. Then work to get better, from all your children.

This kind of expectation is characteristic of good teachers. Many researches have shown that the best teachers believe the children can learn and want to learn. They see each student as an individual and as important, instead of seeing students as types or as groups—i.e., the deacon's kid or bus kids.

These best teachers believe that they can help children learn. To this end they understand the teaching techniques they use and can explain to you what they are doing and why they are doing it that way. They have a drive to share their knowledge with students. They collect things to use in teaching that they read or find in their daily lives. They do this not because the book tells them to do so, but because the children and the teaching are so much on their minds that they can't stop themselves from becoming inveterate collectors. This drive to learn and to share learning is evident in the classroom in the atmosphere the teacher creates. There is an apparent "learning climate" in his classroom. He has good rapport with his students, or in tough situations he has a drive to build such a rapport. He has true empathy with the students; he listens to them, he understands how they feel, and he lets them know he understands. His own personality characteristics seem to activate learning in those around him. He derives great satisfaction from seeing his children learn.

These best teachers are well organized but not overly organized. They can balance organization with flexibility. Though they have high expectations for their children, they can balance that with an acceptance of children as they are. The best teachers are creative. Their teaching lives are charged with a creative energy that does not allow them to travel along last year's rut.

In short, the best teachers put their hearts into teaching.

READING CHECK

1. Recitation, though it has a reputation for being old-fashioned, does still help learning.   T F

2. Recitation and discussion give immediate feedback to the teacher, help the children concentrate, and reinforce the learning.   T F

3. There is no way to have pupil participation in extra-large classes.   T F

4. Activities are not valuable when children plan them.   T F

5. Activities should always be both before and after the main lesson.   T F

6. Science now knows the best ways to teach.   T F

7. It is good planning to have lots of Band-Aid techniques to use when children misbehave.　　T F

8. It is good planning to prevent most misbehavior, rather than treating it after it happens.　　T F

9. Rewards and punishment are effective with children who have little self-discipline.　　T F

10. All children should be treated exactly the same.

　　T F

Appendix

In this section are study helps for each chapter, which can be used when this book is studied in classrooms or in church training groups.

CHAPTER 1: SKETCH OF THE JUNIOR CHILD

Questions *(for discussion or for essay topics)*

1. What memories do you have of your own junior years? What did you like in your classes and clubs? What did you dislike? What failure or disappointment do you remember? What accomplishment? What can you learn from your memories that will help your own teaching?

2. Can you remember a specific time of competition when you were a child? What was its effect on you? Did it motivate? Discourage? How does this incident affect your beliefs about using competition in Christian education?

3. What Scriptural justification can you give for or against using competition?

4. Describe one of the favorite teachers you had as a child. What attributes of that teacher do you try to emulate?

Study Projects

1. Choose a topic important to you and interview several juniors to see what they think or how they think about it. Share your findings with your study group. Topic examples: salvation, heaven, Holy Spirit, drugs,

missions, reading preferences, favorite kind of teacher, favorite classroom activity.

2. Select a passage from a junior Sunday school book and a passage from the Bible. Listen to several juniors read each to you, and assess their word recognition levels according to the following chart.

       a) Independent level: 99 to 100%
       b) Instructional level: 90 to 95%
       c) Frustration level: Below 90%

(A fuller inventory of a child's reading would include, also, a check on the meaning of the words and comprehension of the passage—both literal and inferential. So be cautioned not to make too much of the word recognition score you obtain.)

Observations

1. Observe a junior club in session. What features do the children seem to like? What do they act happy about?

2. Observe a junior Sunday school class. Watch particularly their reading activities. What words do they stumble over? How much difference do you notice between the best readers and the poorest readers?

CHAPTER 2: SPIRITUAL DEVELOPMENT

Questions

1. Can you describe the part conscience played in bringing you to Christ? What part did the Bible play?

2. Are there teachers who helped you along the way in your Christian life? How?

3. Do your own experiences (in 1 and 2 above) help you know how or what you want to teach children?

Study Projects

1. Make your own study of Christian growth in the Bible. What implications do your findings have for our job of teaching children?

2. Interview one or more junior children in depth on a topic chosen from the spiritual development tasks of elementary school years. Try to understand what the children are really thinking. Look behind the words they use and avoid attaching your adult meanings to their words. Write your findings.

Here are some possible goals for the interviews.

What is the child's understanding of:

God
Jesus
church
Bible

What is the child's attitude toward and practice of:

praying
Bible reading
choosing friends
worshiping
Christian service

What is the child's knowledge of:
the Holy Spirit
angels
heaven
hell
sin
salvation

3. After some good experiences on a topic from project number 2, you should be able to devise a questionnaire on that same topic. Obtain responses to your questionnaire from a number of juniors. Others in your class or study group may help you collect a greater number of responses. Compile the results and see what you can learn from them. Your learning may be in the form of a conclusion about the children you studied, or it may be a question that is raised for further study.

CHAPTER 3: MORAL DEVELOPMENT

Questions

1. Do you think that just treatment for people is the highest good we can work for in this life? Why or why not?

2. How do you feel about trying to educate everyone to high stages of moral reasoning? Do you think people will be better off that way?

Study Projects

1. From current news sources collect some quotations from people in public life which have moral dimensions. Discuss these in a class group or small group and try to reach agreement as to which of the three Kohlberg levels each quotation represents.

2. Collect quotations, as above, but from junior children. Categorize them.

3. Read Bettelheim's essay, "Moral Education" in *Moral Education/Five Lectures,* edited by Nancy F. and Theodore R. Sizer. Then write a short essay of your own, relating some of Bettelheim's ideas to your own special field of proficiency. For example, you may relate Bettelheim's ideas to theology, teaching methods, some kind of learning theory or educational philosophy. Or try putting yourself in the place of a parent or teacher of children and agree or disagree with Bettelheim, as seems best to you. Whatever viewpoint you choose be sure it is one you feel comfortable with so you can have genuine, personal reactions to the lecture instead of merely academic ones.

4. Read some other writer on moral education besides Kohlberg and Bettelheim. Write a brief synopsis of the selection you choose, and write a sentence or two giving your personal reaction to or evaluation of it.

CHAPTER 4: DEVELOPMENT OF THINKING

Questions

1. What are some abstractions you think are important for junior children to begin learning? Can you think of ways to make these ideas concrete?

2. How do you feel about using behavioral objectives for junior Bible lessons? Can you cite examples where this worked well?

3. Do you think there is a "spiritual" or other aspect of mind that gets left out when we talk about concrete and abstract thinking? If so, what can you say about its workings?

Study Projects

1. Try the stick experiment with children of several different ages, and try to classify the children in the stages of 1) preoperational, 2) concrete operational, and 3) abstract operational. (Remember this classification is on one problem only and may not hold on other kinds of problems.) To obtain a wider spread of abilities you can include children of primary and junior high ages as well as junior ages.

2. Use the same children you used in project 1 and interview them to see what they think is meant by "Samuel served God" or "do God's will." Try, again, to classify the answers. Do the children understand these in a concrete way, or in an abstract way? Compare the results of this with your results in project 1. Does the kind of thinking that children do on the stick problem tend to predict the kind of thinking they are likely to do on the problems of Bible abstractions?

3. Examine a written lesson or Bible story for juniors and analyze the use it makes of abstract ideas. Do you think it helps to build juniors' understanding of the abstractions or does it assume juniors already understand

them? Explain your conclusions.

4. For a clearer idea of the behaviorist approach to teaching, try this project in small groups or a full class group. First work out one or more well stated behavioral objectives. The standard book on how to do this is *Preparing Instructional Objectives* by Robert F. Mager (Belmont CA, Fearon, 1962). It is essential that each objective state in precise terms 1) what the learner will be able to do, and 2) the criterion for minimum acceptable performance. After your objective is agreed upon, work out a teaching strategy to achieve it. Finally, discuss the result. Is your plan a satisfying lesson? What do you think about building a total Christian education program by this procedure?

CHAPTER 5: UNDERSTANDING METAPHOR

Questions

1. Can you remember hearing parables or fables as a child? What do you remember about their effect on you? (NOTE: Childhood memories often change over the years and, while they may be helpful, they are not entirely trustworthy. See Chapter 4 in the book, *Teaching Primaries,* of this series.)

2. Do you think we should postpone all teaching of Bible analogy until children have learned to handle this kind of reasoning well, or do you think it is better to let children practice and develop their reasoning abilities as they study Bible content? Why?

Study Projects

1. Choose a Bible parable not mentioned in this chapter and decide what action or verb-like emphasis could make it most meaningful to children.

2. Choose a parable or analogy of any kind in the Bible and interview children of various ages to determine their understanding of it.

3. Locate a junior lesson which attempts to teach analogy. What kinds of understandings does it aim for (equivalents of actions, actors, or objects)? Do you think a change of emphasis could make it more meaningful to more children?

4. Read another research study about children's thinking. Report on how the study was conducted and what the findings were.

CHAPTER 6: A MODEL OF LEARNING

Questions

1. Looking back, can you see how discipline or any lack of discipline in your life had its roots in your childhood years and the training you received then? Can you explain and give examples?

2. What do you think about discipline as the basis for learning? Does this seem to fit the way it was in the classes of your childhood or classes that you know of now? Do disciplined children do better at learning than undisciplined children? Does this idea seem to fit with what your common sense tells you?

3. You and your study group share with each other some recent examples of concept, or insight, learning. What information learning was necessary in each case before the new insight could happen?

4. Talk about various classes that you learned a lot in. Was it method that was mainly responsible for the learning? The teacher? Your motivation for learning the subject? Another factor?

5. How does the learning theory in this chapter seem to your commonsense reasoning? Does it describe any of the ways you have learned? Can you give examples? Is it helpful in thinking through something you want to teach to children? What seems right about the theory to you? What problems do you have with it?

6. What are some creative things you have done? Did these happen mostly inside or outside the classroom?

Study Projects

1. Use a lesson of your own or a published lesson, and analyze it according to the three levels of learning. What Level 1 learning does it aim for and is it likely to

achieve? What Level 2 learning? Is there, perhaps, a premature aiming for Level 3 learning without building enough foundation for it?

2. Read and report on a book about any of these topics.

        The brain
        Creativity
        Learning Theory

CHAPTER 7: USING QUESTIONS

Questions

1. Do you think the three-level questioning plan in this chapter should be used with most lessons, or be used only occasionally? Why?

2. In an adult class, after the lesson information is read or presented, do you think it is necessary to follow this junior class plan of repeating the information again with Level 1 questions before asking Level 2 or Level 3 questions? Why or why not?

3. Can you give an example from a class you recently were in of a question that generated a good discussion? What kind of question was it? Did the question lead to learning?

4. What kind of questions do you like to have on a test? Why?

Observation

Observe in a junior class and try to write down each question the teacher uses. Try also to note the kind of interest and response from the children in each case. Comment on what you learn about questions from this observation.

Study Projects

1. Make a tape recording of a junior class and do a more precise study of the questions than may be possible in the observation. List the questions by their three categories. See how many of each the teacher used. What kinds of responses did each kind elicit from the children? How did each kind help their learning? Which questions helped most? Which questions were not successful?

2. Choose a Bible story and write two questions at each of the three levels.

3. Choose a Bible story and write a sequence of questions about it to use in leading a discussion which will help junior age children develop higher thinking skills. Draw a diagram of your questions similar to the one in this chapter, showing how the questions relate to each other.

4. Choose a published lesson and analyze its use of questions. Categorize as many as possible of its questions into Levels 1, 2, or 3. Try to determine whether there is enough knowledge and understanding built at the lower levels before attempting the higher levels.

CHAPTER 8: USING ORGANIZERS

Questions

1. Can you remember any "aha" experience in learning—recent or otherwise? What does it teach you about this kind of experience which learning psychologists speak so much about?

2. Do you have in your head some organizers that help you understand the Bible better? What? Do you have a feeling that you need better organizers? Would you like a Bible scholar to give these to you? Or would you prefer to work them out yourself as your knowledge of the Bible increases?

Study Projects

1. Examine a unit of lessons for juniors. Does it claim to build toward one or more big ideas? How well do you think the lessons will accomplish the claim? What use do they make of some kind of framework? Of flesh for the framework?

2. Invent an organizer for any unit of teaching you wish. Decide what details could be used to give enough meaning to the organizer and what might be safely skipped over in the study of the unit.

CHAPTER 9: USING PUBLISHED CURRICULUM

Questions

1. How should closely graded materials be used in your particular Sunday school? What advantages do you see in this arrangement? What disadvantages?

2. How should departmentally graded materials be used in your Sunday school? What advantages and disadvantages do you see in this arrangement?

3. What has helped you most to learn about your teaching job? In your study group see if there is a difference in this respect between those who started teaching in the last ten years or so and those who have been teaching a long time. (Omit professional teachers from this, and compare only volunteer lay teachers.)

Study Projects

1. Using a unified curriculum, choose at random one or two particular Sundays, and examine the lesson for each age level from nursery through adult. Report on the ways in which it truly is unified and the ways it differs at the various age levels.

2. If your church is using undated materials, find out what is being done to save and reuse some of the items. See if you can improve on the system.

3. Make a plan for your own use in memorizing a chapter of Scripture by the whole method. Try out the plan and keep a log of the process.

4. Plan and carry out an experiment by which your study group could test the comparative efficiency of the whole and the part systems of memorizing.

5. Choose a Scripture portion, and make a series of memory lesson plans showing how you would help a junior class memorize the portion by the whole method.

CHAPTER 10
STYLES IN TEACHING AND DISCIPLINING

Questions

1. On a scale of A to Z (lecture to activities), about where would you place yourself? Why?

2. On the scale of A to Z, what kind of classes do you enjoy the most as a student? Why?

3. Do you think there are differences between adults and children in the amount and kinds of activities needed? Can you give examples of activities that might suit one age but not the other?

4. Do you think the topic of study makes a difference in the way a class should be conducted? Can you back up your answer with an example?

Observation

Observe a junior class. What is your opinion of the value of the activities, discussion, or other pupil participation techniques that you saw? What learning or reinforcement or other values did you see in them? What new knowledge do you think the children took with them from the class?

Study Projects

1. Find a junior lesson which contains one or more activities. Analyze the total lesson and comment on what learning you think the activities will contribute to the lesson.

2. Have one member of your class or study group offer as a case study a discipline problem he has. As a group, work out a plan for handling the problem. If possible, follow up for the next week or two to see what improvement, if any, occurs.

Index

Other books by this author:

Card Packets: